Charles Burchfield.

Portrait by Thomas Hollyman, 1955.

CHARLES BURCHFIELD

BY

JOHN I. H. BAUR

PUBLISHED FOR THE

Whitney Museum of American Art

BY

The Macmillan Company

NEW YORK, 1956

Text by JOHN I. H. BAUR

Curator, Whitney Museum of American Art

Research by ROSALIND IRVINE

Associate Curator, Whitney Museum of American Art

CHRONOLOGY

1893   April 9: born Ashtabula Harbor, Ohio, son of William Charles and Alice (Murphy) Burchfield.

1898   Death of father. Moved with his family to Salem, Ohio. Attended public school and high school. From the seventh grade on, worked after school and Saturdays in a drugstore, then in the mailing department of W. H. Mullins Company.

1911   Graduated from high school; valedictorian of class.

1911-   Accountant, cost department of the Mullins Company.
1912

1912-   Attended the Cleveland School of Art (now the Cleveland Institute of Art). Studied under Henry G. Keller, Frank N. Wilcox and William J. Eastman. Expenses paid by a scholarship and earnings from work at the Mullins plant during vacations.

1915   Began to paint independently.

1916   Summer: worked in cost department of the Mullins Company. Awarded scholarship at the National Academy of Design. To New York City, early October. Left the National Academy after one day in life class. A group of his watercolors exhibited at the Sunwise Turn Bookshop by Mrs. Mary Mowbray-Clarke, who continued to show his work for the next six years. Returned to Salem and the Mullins Company at the end of November. Painted during lunch hours, evenings and weekends.

1918   July: inducted into U.S. Army. Attached to Field Artillery at Camp Jackson, South Carolina; later transferred to the Camouflage Section.

1919   January: discharged from Army with rank of Sergeant. Returned to the Mullins Company. Continued to paint in his spare time.

1920   Summer: devoted full time to painting during a three-month leave of absence from work. Made brief trips to Tennessee and New York.

1921   Fall: moved to Buffalo, N. Y. Became assistant designer, later head of design department, for the wall paper company, M. H. Birge and Sons.

1922   May: married Bertha L. Kenreich of Greenford, Ohio.

1924-   His work handled by the Montross Gallery, New York.
1928

1923   First child, Mary Alice, born. Other children, Martha Elizabeth, born 1924; Sarah Ruth, born 1925; Catherine Esther, born 1926; Charles Arthur, born 1929.

1925   April: moved to Gardenville, N. Y., a suburb of Buffalo, where he still lives.

1929   February: the Frank K. M. Rehn Gallery of New York became his dealer; has continued to handle his work to the present. August: resigned from M. H. Birge and Sons in order to devote full time to painting.

1936   Commissioned by *Fortune* magazine to paint railroad yards at Altoona and Harrisburg, Pa., and the following year to paint sulphur and coal mines in Texas and West Virginia.

1949   Taught summer class at University of Minnesota, Duluth Branch, Duluth, Minn.

1949-1952   Taught special class at Art Institute of Buffalo.

1950   Taught summer class at Ohio University, Athens, Ohio, and again in 1953. Taught summer class at the University of Buffalo, and again in 1951.

1951-1952   Taught advanced seminar, Buffalo Fine Arts Academy.

One-man exhibitions:

1916: Cleveland School of Art; Sunwise Turn Bookshop, N.Y. 1917: Cleveland School of Art. 1918: Laukhuff's Book Store, Cleveland. 1919: Garrick Theater Library, N.Y.; Little Theatre, Cleveland. 1920: Kevorkian Gallery, N.Y. 1921: Art Institute of Chicago; Cleveland School of Art. 1923: Grosvenor Galleries, London, England. 1924: Montross Gallery, N.Y., also 1926 and 1928. 1928: Eastman-Bolton Gallery, Cleveland. 1930: Frank K. M. Rehn Galleries, N.Y., also 1931, 1934, 1935, 1936, 1939, 1941, 1943, 1946, 1947, 1950, 1952 and 1954; Museum of Modern Art, N. Y. (early watercolors of 1916-1918). 1932: Rochester Memorial Art Gallery. 1934: Phillips Memorial Gallery, Washington, D.C. (early watercolors of 1916-1918). 1937: Philadelphia Art Alliance. 1938: Carnegie Institute (retrospective). 1941: Cleveland School of Art. 1944: Albright Art Gallery, Buffalo (retrospective), also circulated by the American Federation of Arts. 1948: Town and Country Gallery, Cleveland. 1953: Cleveland Museum of Art (drawings, retrospective).

Awards and honors:

1921: First Prize in Watercolor and Penton Medal in Silver for Excellence, Cleveland Museum of Art. 1929: Jennie Sesnan Gold Medal, Pennsylvania Academy of the Fine Arts. 1935: Second Prize, Carnegie Institute. 1936: First Prize, Art Association Building, Newport, R.I. 1940: Dana Watercolor Medal, Pennsylvania Academy of the Fine Arts. 1940-1955: Member, Fine Arts Jury, John Simon Guggenheim Memorial Foundation. 1941: Watson F. Blair Prize, Art Institute of Chicago. 1942: Award of Merit Medal, National Institute of Arts and Letters. 1943: Member, National Institute of Arts and Letters. 1944: Chancellor's Medal, University of Buffalo. 1946: L.H.D., Kenyon College, Gambier, Ohio; Philadelphia Watercolor Prize, Pennsylvania Academy of the Fine Arts; Second Honorable Mention, Carnegie Institute. 1947: Dawson Memorial Medal, Pennsylvania Academy of the Fine Arts. 1948-1951 and 1952-1955: Member of the Board of Directors, Albright Art Gallery. 1948: Doctor of Fine Arts, Harvard University; Doctor of Fine Arts, Hamilton College, Clinton, N. Y. 1949-1952 and 1952-1955: Member of the Board of Trustees, American Academy in Rome. 1950: Special Prize, Pennsylvania Academy of the Fine Arts. 1951: LL.D., Valparaiso University, Valparaiso, Indiana. 1952: $500 Award, Metropolitan Museum of Art; James Carey Evans Memorial Prize, Albright Art Gallery. 1955: Sattler's Prize, Albright Art Gallery.

CHARLES BURCHFIELD

Poplar Trees

1916. 20 x 14. Collection of the artist.

FOREWORD AND ACKNOWLEDGMENTS

This book grew out of a retrospective exhibition of Charles Burchfield's paintings and drawings, held at the Whitney Museum of American Art in January and February, 1956. It utilizes the plates and the scholarly material which were in the catalogue of that exhibition, but it adds a much longer biographical and critical text, as well as a number of new illustrations.

Burchfield's life has been uneventful in its outward circumstances but inwardly rich with the creative and emotional experiences of a profoundly romantic personality. Since he was fifteen he has kept a journal, never intended for publication, which is an illuminating record of his thoughts, feelings, struggles and artistic aims over nearly half a century. It requires both generosity and trust to put so intimate a document in the hands of another person, however sympathetic, and I am most grateful to the artist for permitting me to make full use of it. All of the quotations in the following pages are from the journal unless otherwise identified. I have also quoted occasionally from a manuscript of autobiographical notes, which Burchfield kindly prepared to help me with certain aspects of his life and work that were not sufficiently covered in the journal or elsewhere. And I have drawn heavily on the artist's voluminous correspondence with two people, his friend Edward Root, professor of art at Hamilton College, and Frank K. M. Rehn, who was his dealer from 1929 to the present. The Root correspondence is now part of a collection of artists' letters in the Philadelphia Museum of Art, and I am grateful to both Mr. Root and to Mr. Carl Zigrosser of the Museum for permission to use this material. I am equally indebted to Mrs. Frank Rehn and to Mr. John Clancy of the Rehn Gallery for making available not only the letters, but also the lists of paintings, with detailed comments, which Burchfield sent to the gallery with each new shipment of pictures. From these lists have come most of the descriptive notes in the plate section of the book. A few, however, were reprinted by permission from publications of the Albright Art Gallery, the

Fogg Museum of Art, the Museum of Modern Art, and the Newark Museum.

Both Mr. Clancy and the artist have been extraordinarily helpful in the study of the paintings themselves. It must have taken a week to straighten out the small studio at Gardenville after Miss Irvine and I finished looking at the hundreds of unframed watercolors which had formerly been so neatly stored in racks along the walls. By answering endless questions, providing photographs and looking up all kinds of information, they have contributed greatly. Burchfield's own catalogue of his work, compiled with meticulous accuracy in thirteen large volumes, and Mrs. Burchfield's orderly compilation of clippings, reviews and similar material were other inestimable aids. The artist was also kind enough to draw for me detailed maps of Salem and Gardenville, with the country surrounding each, showing his principal sketching grounds in both areas.

I owe a special debt of gratitude to Miss Rosalind Irvine, Associate Curator of the Whitney Museum, who compiled the chronology and bibliography and edited the comments by the artist, which accompany the illustrations. She has helped in a thousand other ways with both the exhibition and the book, neither of which could have been accomplished in the time available without her assistance. To Leona E. Prasse, who organized the comprehensive exhibition of Burchfield's drawings and prints at the Cleveland Museum of Art in 1953, I am indebted for unusually generous advice and practical aid with the artist's graphic work. The chronology and the record of Burchfield's exhibitions and awards in the following pages are based on those in her catalogue, slightly expanded and brought up to date.

Finally, I would like to thank the many collectors, museums and galleries who made their paintings available for the exhibition and permitted them to be reproduced in these pages. Their names appear beneath the illustrations, but special mention must be made of the generosity of Mr. and Mrs. Lawrence A. Fleischman, Mr. William J. Poplack and Mr. John W. Straus who had color plates made of their pictures especially for use here. The Cleveland Museum of Art through its Director, Mr. William M. Milliken, also contributed to new color work.

JOHN I. H. BAUR

I

NORTH: AN INTRODUCTION

...some fabulous Northland unlike any place on earth—a land of deep water-
filled gashes in the earth; old lichen-covered cliffs and mesas, with
black spruce forests reflected in the pools, against which white swans gleam
miraculously. This romantic land of the imagination, the mysterious North
that has haunted me since I was a boy—it does not really exist, but
how did it come into being?

—JOURNAL 1954.

There are three Burchfields in this book.

The first is a young clerk at the W. H. Mullins Company in Salem, Ohio. He has just returned from four years at the Cleveland School of Art and is painting small watercolors during his lunch hours, his evenings and on weekends. They are fantastic watercolors that visualize the song of insects and recreate childhood moods, like fear of the dark; in them, flowers have faces, trees gesticulate and cornstalks dance. At the Mullins Company he never mentions them, for he has no intimate friends at the plant and few outside it. To most of Salem, he is a painfully shy, inarticulate young man who disappears on weekends into Post's Woods and is sometimes seen in the distance by picnickers at The Dutchman's as he fords the Little Beaver Creek and disappears into Trotter's Swamp. The year is 1917.

The second Burchfield is forty-two, married, the father of five children, living in a modest frame house in Gardenville on the outskirts of Buffalo. Six years ago he left his job at the wall paper factory to paint full time, and has managed to support his family, though there have been precarious moments. Already he has made a national reputation with his big watercolors of the industrial scene around him—the shipping in the harbor, the bridges, the railroad yards, the dirty snow clinging to brown, weathered houses. These are entirely different from the fanciful Salem pictures, for they are painted on a larger scale with broad realism, though full of the romantic moods which he senses in the city. He is still a lonely man who makes friends with difficulty and often repels acquaintances by his apparent distance. One day he is sketching on a downtown street. Two boys pass, and one comes nearer to watch him. "You'd better stay away from that guy," says the other. "He's liable to clout you over the head." Do I look so fierce, the artist wonders? It is 1935.

The third Burchfield is living in Gardenville today. He will be sixty-three in April and looks less like an artist than ever. (He reminded one recent interviewer of the family doctor, another of a small-town businessman.) Thirteen years ago, he broke suddenly with the realism of his middle period and abandoned the industrial scene. Now he paints the one subject that has always been closest to his heart—the changing moods and aspects of nature. He paints these in a new style that is a fusion of his early fantastic manner and the great technical resources of his more realist work. It is a style born of the vivid, romantic imagination that has always burned beneath the quietly conventional exterior, a style that transforms even the backyard of suburban Gardenville into images of God's presence in nature. A deeply religious sense of wonder at the miracle of the seasons, of sun and rain, of birth and death in the natural world, has grown in Burchfield through the years. Sketching east of the Bowen Road one day, he left his easel to explore a brook. "I thought, as I squatted on my heels and gazed into the warm amber-colored water with its teeming life, that if one could but read it aright this little watery world would hold the whole secret of the universe. At least I had the feeling I was gazing into infinity."

Oddly, it is the second Burchfield who has been most honored and is still best known, perhaps because his paintings of industrial Buffalo seemed to play a pioneering role in the regional movement which swept American art in the early 1930's and were thus more easily classified and more easily understood. There is scarcely a critic who has not compared his work with the writing of a fellow Ohioan, Sherwood Anderson, generally with the latter's *Winesburg, Ohio.* Burchfield read this book soon after it was published in 1919 and has acknowledged that it made a deep impression on him. There is also no doubt that his work, during these middle years, had at least as much regional flavor as Edward Hopper's paintings, let us say, of New York. (Someone once remarked that Burchfield was only Hopper on a rainy day.) But like Hopper, Burchfield never thought of himself as a regionalist and, as we shall see later, strongly rejected the more militant regional doctrines. Furthermore, he eventually came to feel that the whole realist-industrial phase of his work was a digression, though a fruitful one, from the true direction that he was destined to follow. This direction was the romantic interpretation of nature which drew him instinctively while he was still in art school and which has re-emerged as the dominant aim in his art since 1943. As both his paintings and his journals show, it never entirely disappeared, even in his middle period. It is the durable strand that binds all three Burchfields into one.

Any true understanding of Burchfield and his art must be based on a realization of the intensity of his response to nature. Many academic painters devote themselves to the same theme and produce, at best, only pleasant landscapes and relaxed moods. For Burchfield, nature has always been a mystical experience full of wonders, terrors and true miracles. Every season, every time of day, every change of weather, every flower and insect, even every direction of the compass has its special meaning for him. His feeling for North, though only a single thread in this complex fabric of relationships, may serve to illustrate the consistency and the special quality of his romanticism.

"The old childhood sensation of North," he wrote in his journal in 1917. How it was born he never knew, but from the beginning it was the dark, terrifying, mysterious direction—the heart of the thunderstorm and the blackness of night. It was always to the north that lay those "strange phantom lands" which loomed suddenly in his mind's eye when he was still in art school and had visions of "enormous moonlit cliffs with water roaring at their bases." The crow, for obvious reasons, and August because of its velvety nights and towering thunderheads, were both closely associated with North. So he soon came to think of "the old 'crow-north' feeling," and one of his early watercolors, a garden at night, was called *August North*. All through the middle years, even when he was deeply involved in his paintings of the city, the North feeling would recur without warning. "Over the rim of the earth—to the North—lies the land of the unknown—it is windy, the ground is frozen, hard, barren—there is no snow—white wind clouds scud over a vast gray sky." The mood grew in scope, adding Druidic, primitive, prehistoric associations, but it remained essentially mysterious. Watching the northern lights one night, "I felt as never before the true mysterious nature of 'North'— and knew why it is that the north attracts me, more than any other direction." In Gardenville, for a few unhappy years, he was obsessed with the idea that he had lost all sense of direction, "and with it the elemental side of nature. North—East —South—West do not seem to have their true character." He had a recurring dream of a wooded cave somewhere to the north.

After 1943, when Burchfield returned to painting the moods of nature, North reasserted itself strongly in both his imagination and his art. He had visions like the one quoted at the beginning of this chapter, and once more he tried to introduce the feeling of North in his paintings. Sometimes this was quite unpremeditated; working on his *Song of the Telegraph*, he suddenly found himself creating a new motif, "which just seemed to grow of its own accord . . . a vast cloud in the form of a cawing crow, soaring above the woods to the left and heading due north. It symbolized for me the old yearning of boyhood for the Northlands, beyond the Covered Bridge, evoked by the elemental calls of crows." North entered equally into other pictures like *Sun and Rocks* and *Moonflowers at Dusk*, the latter a new version of his early *August North*. In one way, the mood became more generalized, a feeling for all that was elemental and enduring in nature. But it never entirely lost the undertones of emotion that went back to childhood. Exploring once in wild new territory, the artist was suddenly aware of "the feeling of coming into a Northwoods at twilight. It recalled some vague elusive memory of my boyhood, or was it a dream . . . ? I wish I could grasp the feeling better. . . . Did I experience it, or is it the life-long desire for a dreamwoods?" It still haunts him.

The deep strain of romantic mysticism in Burchfield, of which this is only one instance, has never adequately been recognized. This is due to a number of factors. His reputation as a regional realist and even as a social satirist has tended to obscure his greater body of work in different directions. The fine, moody city-scapes of his middle years deserve, without question, a high rank in his total work, but their many admirers are generally unsympathetic to his more romantic nature painting. On the other hand, there are those critics who feel that his early fantasies of 1916-18 are better than anything he has done since.

To them, Burchfield is a kind of child genius who has not lived up to his promise, and the fantasies themselves, while extraordinary, are after all fantasies—a word that suggests lively imagination but neither profound nor mature emotion. They are indifferent to his realist phase and dislike the later fantasies that he did after 1943, finding them overblown in scale and less spontaneous than those of his youth. So the artist has fallen, critically speaking, between two stools—those who prefer the middle period and those who prefer the early work. No strong voice has yet been raised for the late paintings of his maturity.

In some ways, this is explainable. For a brief period after 1943, Burchfield tried to turn the clock back too literally and to resume the fantastic style and spirit of 1917 as though the middle years had ceased to exist. Almost at once he ran into esthetic difficulties, which are discussed later, but which did indeed mar some of the largest and most publicized work in his new direction. Since then he has abandoned all attempts to be a child again and has used his full technical equipment to embody, in a very personal kind of expressionism, his mature romantic outlook. The romantic spirit, by its nature, is a young one, and in this sense Burchfield has always kept his liaison with youth, as his

Wind and Sunlight in the Woods.
1915. Lead pencil.
16½ x 14¼.
Collection of the artist.

persistent feeling for North can testify. But just as that concept broad-
ened and deepened in meaning, so his art has acquired, in the last
decade, a more profound and elemental romanticism. It is no longer
fantasy in the 1917 sense but a powerful evocation of the mystery and
beauty of God's creation. Some of the greatest pictures of his career—
among them, *Sun and Rocks, An April Mood* and *Night of the Equinox*
—have been painted in only the last six years and are still not widely
known. Yet they mark the crowning achievement, so far, of a painter
who has done more than any other in our day to revitalize the long
American tradition of an intimate and fruitful relation between the
artist and the natural world.

Crickets in November
(New Albany, Ohio). 1917.
Pen and brush with brown ink,
crayon, lead pencil.
11½ x 10⅞.
Collection of Leona E. Prasse.

II

ALONG THE LITTLE BEAVER:
1893-1921

I have never learned to talk and have only listened to the trees.
—JOURNAL 1915

Charles Burchfield was born in Ashtabula, Ohio, April 9, 1893, the son of William Charles Burchfield, a merchant-tailor, and Alice Murphy Burchfield, who had been a school teacher before her marriage. His paternal grandfather was the Reverend James Burchfield, an evangelical preacher known as Hallelujah-Praise-the-Lord Burchfield because, passing once a shop full of people, he had impulsively opened the door and shouted this exhortation at them. His maternal grandfather was a farmer, Ephraim Murphy, descendant of a long line of farmers; the artist's middle name is Ephraim, though he seldom uses it, and then only the initial "E."

When Burchfield was five his father died, leaving the family nearly penniless. His mother took her six children (of whom Charles was the fifth) back to her birthplace in Salem, Ohio, where her relatives proposed to divide them among various branches of the Murphy family. The oldest child, Jim, pleaded for a chance to keep them together, and although he was only fifteen at the time, took a job as coremaker's assistant in a local factory. Two bachelor uncles, Samuel and James Murphy, pooled their savings and bought a six-room frame house on Fourth Street at the northeast edge of town, where the Burchfields lived rent-free. As the other older children grew up, they contributed to the support of the family so that, by the time Charles graduated from high school in 1911, the financial pressure had eased considerably.

Salem, originally settled by Quakers, was then a small manufacturing town of less than ten thousand. The Pennsylvania Railroad ran through the flats on its southern edge, and the drab industrial section was strung out along the tracks. The Burchfields lived on the opposite side of town, at its highest point. There it was almost rural with alleys like country roads between the streets, backyard gardens, sheds and grape arbors. Beyond Fifth Street, a short block away, lay an open, rolling field dominated by "the three trees" which many years later were to become the subject of Burchfield's nostalgic painting for the Salem library. Cutting across the field, past Brooks' mansion, you could turn right on Painter Road and soon find yourself at the edge of Post's Woods, the heart of Burchfield's private and enchanted empire, bordered on the north by Pine Hollow and the Covered Bridge, on the south by Bentley's and Farquhar's Woods, on the east, beyond the Egypt Road, by Trotter's Swamp, The Dutchman's, Bloodroot Hollow and that stream which threads its way through all his later recollections of youth, the middle fork of the Little Beaver.

Every spring would come the day when his mother would let him take off his high-topped shoes and long black stockings—"then the delicious, incredible sensation of . . . feet sinking in the lush cool grass." With his lunch and his dog—a pug—he would be off to the country for the day, sometimes berrying or swimming with friends, more often alone, exploring, collecting pollywogs, minnows, butterflies and other insects or digging plants for his wildflower garden under the grape arbor at home. "From the 6th grade to 3rd year in High School, I was without an intimate friend," he later wrote in his journal, and a pattern of aloneness, which sometimes grew into an aching loneliness, seems to have been established in these years. But he also discovered its counter in the infinite solace of nature, the peace that filled him when he slipped away to Post's Woods and stood listening to the wind in the trees or traced the intricate windings of the Little Beaver for miles north to New Albany and beyond. A passionate desire to understand nature, to be on intimate terms with her complex patterns, led him at times in an almost scientific direction. During his junior year at high school, he undertook to record all the local wildflowers and blossoming fruit trees. Not content with single blooms, he made huge bouquets of each, which he drew in meticulous detail. The effort, coupled with his school work, brought on a collapse of several weeks. "It was termed 'brain fever' by the doctor," he says, "but I wonder now if it would not be called simply nervous exhaustion."

From the seventh grade on, Burchfield worked after school and Saturdays doing odd jobs for a local drugstore. In his last year of high school he worked the same hours in the mailing department of the W. H. Mullins Company, a metal fabricating plant which had produced, as well as automobile parts, Saint-Gaudens' copper figure of Diana for the Metropolitan Tower in New York. Like many lonely children, he read much, ranging from Horatio Alger stories and *The Rover Boys* to *Alice in Wonderland*, Mark Twain and *Robinson Crusoe*. He was devoted all his life to that wonderful saga of the adventures of Mole, Rat and Toad—Kenneth Grahame's *Wind in the Willows*. And perhaps the greatest influence on his early art, though largely unconscious, were the illustrations in *St. Nicholas* magazine and the mood of the Grimm Brothers' fairy stories.

Burchfield painted and drew before he entered the first grade. His youthful admirations were diverse and included, oddly enough, the fashionable illustrations of Charles Dana Gibson, who years later made the presentation of Burchfield's gold medal at the American Academy of Arts and Letters. But his greatest favorites were the animal illustrations of Charles Livingston Bull, which he would copy, then color to his own taste. From the beginning, he showed a decorative flair that found expression in the embellishment of school maps and in his first original designs, a series of rosettes done in the sixth grade.

Burchfield's decision to become an artist—his original thought was to be an illustrator—met with nothing but sympathy at home. ("I believe my mother is a genius," he wrote gratefully in his journal a few years later.) A scholarship of $120, awarded on his graduation from high school in 1911, was too slim a capital to take him to art school, so he went back to the Mullins Company as a full time filer of automobile parts. It was hard, disagreeable work, but he stuck to it until he came down with typhoid fever, and after his recovery he continued to work there at a less strenuous job in the cost department. His spare time was spent, as before, in wandering over the countryside in all weather. It was this year that he read *Walden*, Thoreau's journals and everything he could find by John Burroughs, whose observations and style he unconsciously imitated in his own journals. For a moment he considered abandoning art to become a nature writer.

By the fall of 1912, Burchfield had saved enough money to enter

the Cleveland School of Art (now the Cleveland Institute of Art), but
for the four years he was there he had to spend every Christmas and
summer vacation working in the Mullins plant. At Cleveland, the first
two years were devoted to general studies, the last two to an Illustra-
tion Course, although half way through it he decided "to be an artist
and just paint pictures." His feelings about the school, both then and
afterwards, were mixed. He hated cast and life drawing and for years
felt that he had never learned to draw. Nor could he find among his
teachers much response to his own romantic feeling for nature. "I do
not think there is an artist in the school," he wrote during his last year
there, "to feel the beauty and poetry of nature as existing for its own
sake."

On the other hand, there were several teachers—notably Henry G.
Keller, Frank N. Wilcox and William J. Eastman—who gave him much.
Writing of Keller later (*Magazine of Art*, September 1936), Burchfield
said, "One of the most significant things a teacher can do for his students is to arouse their curiosity, not only about the art of painting . . .
but also about the other arts, and life in general as well." Keller would
analyze the structure of the *Arabian Nights* and discourse on Russian
ballet. He was enthusiastic about Oriental art and talked vaguely, but
sympathetically, of the modern movements which had recently made
so large a stir in the Armory Show. He did not, however, introduce
his pupils to the work of the European modernists, and it was many
years before Burchfield saw a Cézanne, Van Gogh or Picasso. On the
other hand, he did become acquainted with Chinese painting and
Japanese prints, of which his favorite masters were Hiroshige and
Hokusai. At Keller's urging, he went to the Diaghilev Ballet on its
first tour of America and was enthralled with Nijinsky and Pavlowa
and the costume designs of Bakst.

Burchfield's taste turned consistently toward the exotic, the decorative and romantic. In his first year he was carried away by the "Egyp-
tian Festival" which the Design Department organized to celebrate
the thirtieth anniversary of the school. He admired such illustrators
of fairy stories as Edmund Dulac, Arthur Rackham and especially
the Russian, Ivan Yakovlevich Bilibin, "whose flat, decorative conventionalizations of landscape fascinated me." He was swept off his feet
by Wagner—though the enthusiasm did not last very long—and fell

in love with Stravinsky's *Petrouchka* and Rimsky-Korsakov's *Scheherazade*. He read Yeats, the *Rubaiyat of Omar Khayyam* and once, while recovering from an appendectomy, a huge volume of Hindu mythology, which confounded one of his nurses. "You don't look like that kind of a fellow," Burchfield says she remarked, adding, himself, "I don't know just what she meant."

Yet perhaps that nurse was the first person to sense the paradoxical quality in Burchfield's character—the romantic spirit behind the sober, conventional exterior. She would have been more astonished if she had happened to see him one wild February day that last year in Cleveland, running and dancing alone through a blizzard, intoxicated by its force and beauty. Nothing in Burchfield's appearance or social behavior gave the barest hint of the dreams and fantasies which were beginning to possess his mind as his creative powers developed. Desperately shy, tortured, as he was to be for many years, by real or imagined social blunders, diffident and difficult in his relations with others, he never played the role of the bohemian artist and looked (though he was not) more at home behind his desk in the Mullins Company than at an easel. Only in the journals, and soon in the paintings, can a different Burchfield be seen. "I walk in a maze of dream worlds, oblivious to all beings and things," he wrote early in 1916. And a few days later: "While working in Life [Class] this morning, I suddenly thought of all the dreams I have ever had of wildflowers and unseen woods, and a great longing came over me to live in such a dream world, meeting no other being. I became so oblivious to my surroundings and self that I grew dizzy."

He worried about earning a living and about his romantic attachment to a young woman in the school. "In seeming endless chain my mind thrashes out landscape problems; the advantages of matrimony, what is the role of friendship, whether to make a sketch or not; the hatred of dogmas; should not an artist become a hermit; the futility of method; the sordidness in people's faces; self detestation; composition of weird music; is there anything beautiful in love?—and finally, what controls the mind?" These, or doubts like them, assail the young everywhere, but in Burchfield's case they were intensified by his loneliness. Sometimes there would be "a morning and afternoon of almost unbearable gloom. Plans for suicide ran through my head." But then, at evening, he "wandered through Lakeview cemetery under the moon —and renewed a thousand sensations and felt the beauty of life."

In June, 1916, Burchfield graduated from the Cleveland School and returned to Salem and his job in the cost department at Mullins. For about a year he had been painting his own impressions of nature—at first in rather harsh, brilliant colors and bold, flat patterns; then, in 1916, with quieter tones, greater subtlety and more poetic feeling, though still in an essentially flat and decorative manner. Now he spent every spare moment sketching in the familiar countryside of his youth, and a wave of happiness came over him. "After a long period of gloom . . . and self-hatred, I came home tonight under the half-moon exceedingly light of heart, so that I unconsciously whistled." Fireflies "popped like stars" in the marshy valleys, and as he walked he composed strange music to an improvised tale of unhappy lovers. He had no more possessions, he reflected, than the love of nature and life, but then, "the true poet needs no more." For was he not an artist these days, sketching when and where he wished, with the whole world of nature still to be explored? Its bigness overwhelmed him. With youth's unconscious egotism, "life seemed short for the stupendous work I am to accomplish."

The interlude was broken by news that the Cleveland School had obtained a scholarship for him at the National Academy of Design in New York. Burchfield was doubtful—"Can a caged bird fly even if let loose . . . ?" But the opportunity seemed important, and early in October he went. It was not a happy experience. One visit to the Academy's life class convinced him that he was through with schools forever, and he did not return. A sparrow's song made him homesick for the marshes; he felt spiritually dead and wrote in his journal, "I can find no reason for staying here." But stay he did, until late in November. One reason was the modest success that he had with a group of watercolors which he had brought with him from Salem. At a friend's suggestion, he took these to the Montross Gallery, which offered to hold them in a portfolio and sell them for $25 each. At the last minute, Burchfield could not bear to part with them, but through Mr. Montross he met Walter Pach, who persuaded the young artist to show his work to Mary Mowbray-Clarke at the Sunwise Turn Bookshop, then at 2 East 31st Street.

Mrs. Clarke was enthusiastic, exhibited his pictures in her store, sold several to clients and bought one or two herself. Burchfield spent hours there, trying to forget his homesickness, and has always been grateful to her for launching him on his professional career.

He was rooming at this time with a former classmate, Frank Daniels, and both of them were perennially out of funds. Burchfield tried a variety of jobs. The longest—air-brushing Christmas decorations for a department store—lasted a week; he spent one night operating the switchboard of an electric sign on Broadway, one day as a toy designer before he was discharged for incompetence. Often their only meals were rolls and coffee. By the middle of November, Burchfield wrote in his journal, "This seems a crisis in my life. Without money, discouraged, I look myself over. I lack the courage to do the hard work. I dream ideas and possibilities, I see the mountain tops but I haven't the character to climb. . . . Failure looms." A day or two later, he met Howard Coluzzi, another artist, at the bookshop. "It's better to go back home," Coluzzi advised him, "get a job, any kind of a job, and paint in your spare time. That way you are absolutely independent." Mrs. Clarke urged him to stay and shortly afterwards sent him the encouraging news of the sale of another watercolor (which Burchfield is sure she bought herself). It was too late. He had already written home for the loan of his railroad fare and welcomed the sale only as a means of repaying the loan. By the end of November, he was back in Salem.

Burchfield's deep sense of failure, which oppressed him all the way home, evaporated in the warmth of his family's welcome and the immediate willingness of the Mullins Company to give him back his old job. But "I had two days before I started to work," he recalls in his autobiographical notes, "and although it was snowing I went sketching out into the country. One of the supremely happy moments of my whole life was when I stood in the woods and listened to the wind soaring in the tree-tops. After the days of agony in New York, it seemed to me the most wonderful music I ever heard. The result of that day's walk was six watercolors, done in the evenings of the following week. . . . I was home spiritually as well as physically."

The next year-and-a-half produced Burchfield's finest early paintings —that group of small watercolors interpreting nature's moods and sounds and the emotions evoked by them in childhood—works which were destined to be half forgotten, then rediscovered, and which would finally bring him his first national reputation when they were exhibited at the Museum of Modern Art in 1930. But at the moment he had put aside completely the search for fame, and in later years he often wished that he could paint as naturally, as spontaneously as he now did. Most of his work was done in the evenings and on weekends, but some was even crowded in at noon. He had an hour and a half for lunch, allowed half an hour to walk to and from the office, fifteen minutes to eat, which left forty-five minutes to do a quick sketch. The material for his evening painting was gathered on his walks between home and factory, which doubtless explains why so many of his subjects were drawn from alleys and backyards. Often, at night, he had to splash cold water in his eyes to keep awake.

All of these watercolors—both the decorative 1916 papers and the moodier ones of 1917—were based first of all on a very exact observation of nature, incorporated in both sketches and journal entries. He would note "how the big wind's course over the land was marked by sudden isolated waving of trees in rapid succession," that the immensity of sky could be suggested by a small area as effectively as by a large, that the same sapling which gleamed white against a house looked like a black claw against the sky. He was often in despair at the inadequacy of art before the "big epic power of nature," and exhorted himself to subjugate his painting to nature's own poetry, "not invent a quasi poetry and try to twist the facts of nature around to it."

Burchfield never consciously abandoned this ideal, but his own response to nature was so deeply subjective, so imbued with romantic feeling, that he seems to have been quite unconscious of transferring his personal moods to the world around him. His sensitive imagination turned easily in a morbid direction. "One night last week I lay in bed fearing to go to sleep for fear I would wake in insanity." And often, as he sat in his room, "out of the corner of my eye I see something run past—I look but see nothing." In the woods, particularly at dusk or after nightfall, the mood heightened. Just before he went to New York, he wrote in his journal, "I do not wander the woods free of superstition any more. Something seems to be lurking behind stumps or writhing logs—flowers have faces, but they are not always pleasant." One

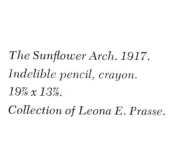

The Sunflower Arch. 1917.
Indelible pencil, crayon.
19⅞ x 13⅞.
Collection of Leona E. Prasse.

January evening, soon after his return, he took a "night walk over luminous fields—a wild wind out of southwest—I entered Post's Woods, fascinated by its awfulness, but fled away in terror; as I had [stood] looking where nothing was, two stumps suddenly appeared; the black north was awful." There was no foretelling when the mood would recur. One peaceful twilight he stopped by a little pond, struck by sudden fear at the reflection of ghostly stumps in the still water—"at once a tremendous ringing and pounding commenced in my ears—growing louder and louder—though this ringing was terrific, yet the woods seemed absolutely silent—from somewhere a strange bell (such as is used in Chinese music) commenced—I was too overcome to take note of anything—finally a familiar farm sound broke the spell and I relaxed, in a cold sweat, and continued my way homeward." Sometimes he dreamed of evil faces in trees, with limbs like clutching hands, and once he composed in his journal a fantasy of a man pursued by the forest, which beat at his door with its branches and finally invaded the house.

Not that the mood was always macabre. Finding a dead morning-glory blossom precariously balanced on a frond of grass, he thought, "My most vagrant imaginings can't approach the poetry of the sight of this queer occurrence." Often he felt an exultant freedom as the wind roared through the trees and the big clouds sailed across the moon. He liked "a wild ragged night" and would lie awake listening to the boom of the town clock and the rattle of rain in the rainspouts. Sounds and music moved him nearly as much as sight. As he walked, he would compose music in his mind, and one icy February night he danced in the fields to "music that was so wonderful the hearers for-got where they were, or that it was music, and when it was ended they were still carried on and on into strange realms." The sound of wind in the telegraph wires gave him an elysian feeling as if it came from the infinite depths of the sky, and the "telegraph harp" haunted him all his life until he finally painted it in 1952. The song of birds, insects, spring peepers, the noise of church bells and factory whistles all had special meanings, and as early as 1916 he wondered whether "queer accidental noises, such as the creaking of a wagon on a cold day or the sound of a pail of water being hit sharply could be conventionalized and put into musical compositions," little realizing that within a year he would be attempting to do this in the infinitely more difficult field of painting.

All of these moods were related in some degree to Burchfield's child-hood, to the naive, unquestioning acceptance of spirits and presences in nature which he had had in his youth. A sharp nostalgia for the experiences of boyhood assailed him, as it has at intervals throughout his life. It began about 1916, when he was still in art school. Sitting on a warm hillside one March day, a flood of nearly forgotten sensa-tions came over him. "I seemed to view life with the old romantic eye of boyhood when love was a thing holy and life contained nothing but musing on hilltops." After his return from New York—partly, perhaps, in reaction to that unhappy time, partly because he found himself painting again in the familiar setting of his childhood—this nostalgia deepened and became, as he later wrote, almost an obsession. Once, he started for Post's Woods about sundown to sketch. "As I walked out in the golden haze I saw nature with the old eye of my boyhood; entering the woods, distracting sensations seized me—I felt a thrill from the woods but could not grasp it quite; on all sides wonderful things were taking place and I only half comprehended. Nightfall was terrible."

The formidable task which Burchfield undertook between the latter part of 1916 and the first few months of 1918 was the translation of these elusive moods into pictorial form. Unlike most romantic painters, he did not depend on the half-defined and the suggestive, but worked from the beginning with clarity and precision. The style which he had evolved in his last year at school was flat, calligraphic, sometimes almost poster-like, but it lent itself to fanciful interpretations of purely natural phenomena, as in the exaggerated pattern of the bark in *Poplar Trees.* While this picture is principally decorative, Burchfield soon discovered that the same style could be used, with certain innovations, for more romantic ends. Chief of these innovations was the double image, the use of natural objects painted to be easily recognizable yet also to resemble something else—often a sinister something else. Flowers become odd, small creatures in a garden at dusk. The shadow beneath a bush is transformed into a cave or a gaping mouth. In *Ghost Plants,* the spaces between the leaves of the cornstalks are eyes, and the stalks themselves dance an ungainly Virginia reel. Exaggeration of size and proportion is used to create a variety of effects from the morbid atmosphere of *Garden of Memories* to the raffish one of *Rogue's Gallery.*

Most of these paintings are closely related to his earlier work in their flat patterns, which retain a decorative quality despite the change of emphasis. But in 1917, Burchfield began to deepen his space and work in a freer, less calligraphic manner. Still more important were his

From "Conventions for Abstract Thoughts." 1917. Pencil. Collection of the artist.

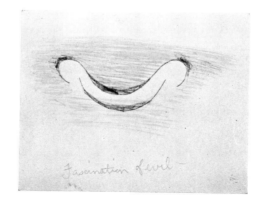

experiments in devising a series of abstract shapes which would symbolize various moods and which, by their very character, would evoke
emotion both more subtly and more powerfully than the double image.
In a notebook, which he called *Conventions for Abstract Thoughts,*
he drew some twenty motifs of this kind, many of them with free variations, representing a range of predominantly gloomy moods such as
Fear, Morbidness, Dangerous Brooding, Insanity, Menace, Fascination of Evil. These were to appear in several of his 1917-18 paintings
and have also run, though with less precise symbolism, through much
of his recent work. In their appropriateness, their inventiveness and
their concentrated vitality, they were an extraordinary accomplish-
ment for so young an artist.

How did these symbols originate? Not by pure invention, Burchfield
insists, but in most cases from visual experience. Sometimes this is
fairly obvious. Insanity and Imbecility are both staring eye motifs, and
Fear seems to have evolved from the same source, although it ended as
a hooked spiral. Fascination of Evil is plainly a smiling mouth, and
Menace is apparently a mouth of a more sinister character. To this
writer there is also a suggestion that the forms of Morbidness and Morbid Brooding came from those fairy-book illustrations which Burch-

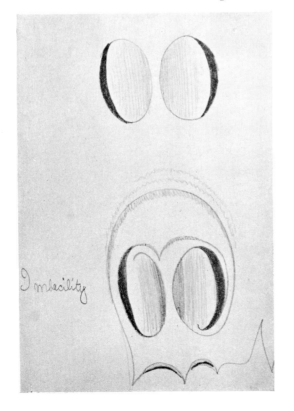

From "Conventions for Abstract Thoughts." 1917.
Pencil. Collection of the artist.

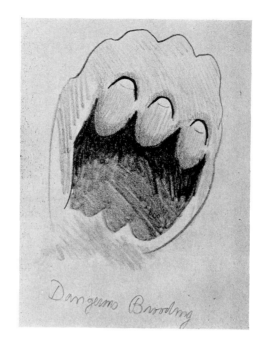

*From "Conventions for Abstract Thoughts." 1917.
Pencil. Collection of the artist.*

field loved as a child and still admired in art school; they seem to be a profile of the fantastically peaked and sway-backed houses that all witches inhabit, and the artist frequently applied the same shape to his own haunted houses.

Burchfield's use of these symbols can be most clearly demonstrated in one of his finest early paintings, *Church Bells Ringing—Rainy Winter Night,* painted in December, 1917. Its genesis was in childhood recollections of the terrifying booming of a church bell on a wild winter night, an emotion which returned to him one November evening as he lay in bed listening to the pealing. But like all his work of this nature, it was also based on careful observation and a conscious effort to reconstruct all the shadings of that early emotion. On November 8, he went down to the Baptist Church, sketched the steeple and noted in his journal its hawk-like aspect. Passing it a week later, he decided that it looked more like a grotesque parrot. On December 5, wanting to get the full impact of the sound, "I wandered between the Baptist and Presbyterian Church waiting to hear the bells ring—I ran back to one too late—the other I arrived at in time to hear the last ponderous beats—the whole tower seemed to vibrate with a dull roar afterwards, dying slowly and with a growl."

With these preparations, he embarked on the painting, making full use of the newly devised abstract symbols. The parrot's head has the

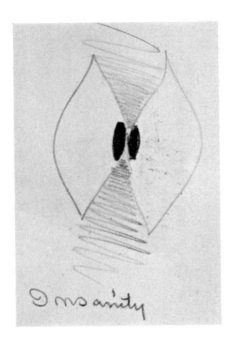

Insanity

From "Conventions for Abstract Thoughts." 1917.
Pencil. Collection of the artist.

eyes of Imbecility. The hooked spiral of Fear is emblazoned on the tower and repeated in the sky. The peaked form of Morbidness is the shape of the house at the right and of its doors and windows, while high on its wall is the smiling mouth of Fascination of Evil. The house at the left seems happier, though only, perhaps, by contrast. There is a Christmas tree in one window and a brightly burning candle in another, but the windows themselves are in the domed form of Melancholy, and the door panels bear the crossed eyes which meant variously Meditation or Insanity.

It would be a mistake, however, to interpret these symbols too rigidly, for Burchfield never intended them as a literary key to his meanings. They are, rather, evocative pictorial elements which he varied, altered and wove together as the mood and the design required. Here, for instance, the fear motif in the sky has been stretched into great waving bands to suggest the noise of the bells reverberating through the dark. In another picture, *The Night Wind*, the same motif becomes part of the wild gale sweeping across the heavens, while a second symbol from the notebook, the sightless eyes of Imbecility, is transformed into the threatening mask of night. Nor was Burchfield's formal language limited to the devices in the notebook; these were the commonest, but in every picture he added new forms to meet individual requirements, like the parrot on the Baptist Church, the upflung wing in *The Night Wind* or the bizarre stumps in *Snow Storm in the Woods*.

Burchfield's style varied considerably in the 1917 papers, and seems to have been controlled largely by the nature of his subjects. When he tackled the difficult problem of insect noises—a theme which absorbed him in several pictures—he returned instinctively to a more calligraphic manner and used a repeated pattern of wiry V's and spirals to suggest the shrilling of crickets and katydids by mapping, as it were, their leaps and gyrations. On the other hand, certain sunlit summer landscapes, like *Dandelion Seed Balls and Trees* or *Poplars in June*, are much more broadly painted with an energetic system of strokes which suggests Van Gogh, although Burchfield was quite ignorant of his work at the time. By the sheer character of his drawing he even transformed the Victorian interior of his mother's house into a kind of rich and moody decoration.

Since he knew nothing of the modern expressionists or futurists, to whom he bears a certain resemblance, where did Burchfield find the diverse elements of this flexible, expressive, yet decorative style? Partly, without question, from Oriental art, to which Keller had introduced

From "Conventions for Abstract Thoughts." 1917.
Pencil. Collection of the artist.

him at school. In addition to his admiration of Japanese prints, he had also seen, in 1913, some Chinese scroll paintings. In the spring of 1915, while he was on vacation in Salem, he had gone out to "the three trees" one evening to sketch the sunset, and while he was there a sudden idea had come to him; he would paint, in continuity, transitions of weather and seasons, such as the development of a thunderstorm from a clear day, followed by a brilliant moonrise. Each phase would be a separate picture, but the pictures would be so designed that they could be united in a single composition. Hundreds of drawings were made, which he called all-day sketches, but the project was never completed. Perhaps its most interesting aspect is that, in 1915, Burchfield thought of his idea as entirely original and did not realize until many years later that it undoubtedly had its genesis in the scroll paintings. In the same way, Oriental art may have influenced him unconsciously in other fields than continuity, especially in his calligraphic line, his conventionalization of natural forms and his personification of natural forces.

Yet oddly enough, there is very little Oriental flavor in Burchfield's painting. More often it had a distinctly mid-Victorian, "Gothick" quality, and to Alfred Barr, who wrote the foreword to the Museum of Modern Art's 1930 exhibition, it suggested "the influence of the silhouettes, the textures, the Spencerian flourishes, the very wall-papers and stained glass of the mid-nineteenth century." To these one might add the more verifiable influences of the *art-nouveau* style of *St. Nicholas* magazine, the fairy-book illustrators, especially Rackham whose grotesque trees with human faces may have been the forebears of Burchfield's haunted forests, and perhaps even the costume designs of Bakst—all known enthusiasms of his. But influences are elusive in Burchfield's case because he was quite unaware of them himself. Nor is there evidence that any single one was decisive in his development. He assimilated them all subconsciously and went on to forge, in those lonely weekends and lunch hours, a style that was among the most original of his generation.

In July, 1918, Burchfield was called for Army service and sent to Camp Jackson, South Carolina, for training in the Field Artillery. At first he was unhappy, confused, his mind in "utter chaos," but life improved when he was transferred to the camp's Camouflage Section,

under the command of Lieutenant William Yarrow. The work was
more congenial and there were even incidents with a certain humor,
such as the visit of a certain major, who became infuriated by the
stench of a dead mule which the camouflage men were casting and
spurred his horse over one of their artificial hills—a maneuver that demolished weeks of work and nearly demolished the major. Yarrow was
an artist himself (he later painted a mural for Princeton), and he occasionally let Burchfield off to sketch in the surrounding country where,
for a time, he "became lost in Negro Fairyland." Shortly after his dis-
charge in January, 1919, the haunted, poverty-stricken back-country of
the South found expression in a few strange little drawings, and in one
similar watercolor, *Haunted Evening*. These, more than any of his other
work, suggest fairy-book illustrations.

Returning to Salem, Burchfield resumed his job at the Mullins Company and his solitary painting. But now everything seemed changed.
His work galled him; "there is nothing so dispiriting as routine," he
wrote in his journal. He suffered from "hideous self-consciousness," from
"morbid or melancholy thoughts," from spells of intense misanthropy:
"I awoke in the morning despising all mankind." He conceived a strong
dislike of the church and organized religion. Only nature still had the
power to comfort him, and for a time he tried desperately to re-estab-
lish his intimate relation with her, conceiving the idea of a series of
paintings devoted to the feelings of birds, their thoughts, emotions and
how the world looked to them. Of the results, Burchfield wrote nine
years later (in his article *On the Middle Border*), "There followed a degeneracy in my art that I have never been able to explain. . . . I later
destroyed all the paintings of this period...viewed from any angle what-
soever, there is not a single redeeming feature about them—and I may
add that vagaries of the Da-da school were nothing compared to mine
at this time, though I had never heard of Da-daism then." Today, he
regrets this destruction, and at the writer's request, he reconstructed
from memory some of the 1919 papers in pencil sketches. These do
not, of course, shed much light on the style of the lost pictures, but they
show that the subjects were chiefly nature fantasies such as a sleeping
bird through which, as if transparent, one can see an unlaid egg and
within it a curled embryo. In another paper, birds rise in startled flight
and a flame-like pattern from flooded woods; again, a flock of blue-

birds leaves the imprint of their color on the trees. Not all the subjects were birds. Blooming branches sprout mysteriously from old brick kilns; dead stumps take the form of skulls and prehistoric skeletons. Except for the interpretation of bird-thoughts, most of these paintings do not seem strikingly different from the fantasies of 1917, though they were doubtless less successful. Mary Mowbray-Clarke told him they looked like caricatures of his earlier work, a description that he decided was very apt.

Perhaps another reason that Burchfield felt they represented a degeneracy was that, even before he entered the Army, he had begun to put this kind of fantasy behind him and to paint the contemporary scene in Salem and in surrounding mining villages like Teegarden. In May, 1919, Richard Laukhuff, proprietor of a Cleveland bookstore, gave him a copy of Sherwood Anderson's *Winesburg, Ohio.* Reading it, the artist felt a growing conviction that his imaginative nature paintings were a blind alley and that he must now commit himself wholly to the realities of Middle Western life, though even in this field a strong element of romantic fancy continued for a time to color his attitude. From the beginning of his mature career, Burchfield had been fascinated with houses. "A house is often more moody than nature," he wrote in 1916. "They are built by men as dwellings . . . and this strange creature results. In the daytime they have an astonished look; at dusk they are evil; seem to brood over some crime. . . . Each one is individual." Some, he thought, had fishy eyes, some an air of silent expectancy, some a look of insanity. By 1920, he had come to feel that houses symbolized the lives they sheltered, and he filled his journal with written character sketches of the inhabitants of houses he planned to paint.

So when he reached the decision to put childhood moods and memories behind him, it was to houses that he turned as the best vehicle for the expression of contemporary life. All the bitter drabness of the industrial West is in these pictures. Shabby miners' huts seem to be settling wearily into the raw mud, their windows like bleary, sightless eyes. Gaunt black houses on a back street have porches like mouths and an air of awkward ferocity. He painted these "old houses, older than even the hills they stand on, squalor of poverty within"—in a new style, the brushstrokes harsh and heavy, the color sooty or acid. Grays and blacks predominate; skies are a dirty yellow, sometimes an electric-blue shadow clashes with the surrounding drabness. Another theme that fascinated him was the abandoned coal mines and coke ovens that dotted the country around Salem; in his pictures they gape like angry wounds in the scarred earth.

It is not surprising that Henry McBride called these pictures songs of hate when they were shown in Burchfield's first one-man exhibition in New York at the Kevorkian Gallery in 1920. (McBride also called him a "young hyena" and said he "yawped like a lusty infant.") Burchfield was pleased at the success of the exhibition, but distressed at the

A Dying Town. 1919.
Pen and India ink,
India ink wash.
5⅜ x 8¾.
Collection of
the artist.

suggestion that he hated Salem. Just a few months before the review appeared, he had been standing by the back window at noon, watching the snow fall and thinking to himself, "the old grape arbor, the dead bush, the crude yellow and red houses—how good it seems they exist." It was not Salem that was wrong, but himself. The pictures were a reflection of the dark mood that had possessed him just before he went into the Army and that had persisted through much of 1919. Now his mood was changing, and with the change Salem took on a fairer aspect. On October 10, 1919, he wrote in his journal, "I feel happy today in the reality of things—that the rain pattering on the roof can be heard, that half bare trees are visible against the bare sky." Three days later he was grateful "for the laughter of people, for tall

Apple Orchard. 1920.
Pen and India ink,
India ink wash,
lead pencil
indications.
11¾ x 17⅞.
Collection of
Leona E. Prasse.

brick chimneys sending smoke up into the solemn air, for the hoarse wheeze of a locomotive." In the margin, by the first entry, he has recently noted that this passage marks perhaps his "first glimmerings of maturity."

New pictures began to throng his mind, and painting seemed a pleasure again. He explored a number of deserted coal mines at considerable bodily risk, and coming out, was struck by "the startled white world." At Hanover, he jotted down his impressions: "huge square-like stores—men clustered at entrance to a livery stable—woman on a porch, little girls parading in their Sunday dresses; boys quarreling around an auto; popular song jingle; geometrical holes where fire has burned out a building, full of bricks and tin—June sunlight pouring over [everything]—catbird singing in some neighborhood." At Wellsville, where "the gaunt unpainted houses fairly 'whine,'" he sketched the railroad yards, taking a new pleasure in the locomotives with their plumes of smoke and their hoarse whistles. All kinds of houses continued to fascinate him; buying lard for his mother at a nearby farm, the primitive rooms and gaping doorways set him to dreaming of what it would be like to sit there in the deathly hush before a snowstorm, one's mind a blank, listening to the clock tick.

The watercolors that followed were not, at first glance, so very different from those of 1918-19. They were still painted with a rather coarse stroke, still quite monochromatic, especially a series of winter scenes done in cold blues and grays. The spirit, however, was different. There was no attempt to disguise drabness and squalor where they existed, but they were no longer the dominant notes. Burchfield was seeing his subjects with a more sympathetic eye, discovering picturesque beauty in objects as diverse as false-front stores and railroad engines, sensing, too, the dying frontier quality of Salem, the nostalgia of abandoned and outdated things. Sometimes he tried to emphasize his poetic feeling by veiling the harshness of the scene in snow or dusk; in one strange picture, *Spring Twilight,* the ugly little town is framed between a pond reflecting the moon and a frieze of branches which seems to have trapped the oncoming night in a pure cubist pattern. More often he preferred to paint with vigorous realism, shying away from the obvious expression of mood and letting his subjects speak for themselves. As part of this trend, he became increasingly interested in light, studied the way it fell on old clapboard houses and, in one unusual picture, *The Thunderclap,* built his whole composition with dramatic lighting. "The faithful interpretation of natural truth," he wrote, "should be a matter of religion—even a bud on a twig wrongly placed would be a sin."

After the Kevorkian exhibition in 1920, Burchfield had made enough money in sales to enable him to take a three-month leave of absence

Spring Rain
(West Main Street,
Salem, Ohio). 1920.
Brush and India ink,
India ink wash,
lead pencil.
6⅞ x 10½.
Collection of Mrs.
Marguerite Munger.

from the Mullins Company. Part of this time was spent painting in Tennessee, where he experimented with gouaches of sky effects. (*The Thunderclap* was one of these.) He also fitted in a brief trip to New York in September, where he met Arthur B. Davies, who tried to interest him in a new oil-tempera technique. He had hardly returned to his job at Salem when the minor depression of 1921 struck, and he found himself out of work. At first this seemed providential, since he still had some money and could now devote his whole time to painting. He was further encouraged when a jury of the Cleveland Society of Artists, headed that year by George Bellows, awarded him first prize. He does not even seem to have worried about his precarious financial situation when, early that spring, he fell in love with Bertha Kenreich, daughter of a farmer in nearby Greenford, whose family had long been friends of the Burchfields. Instead, he dreamed the spring away, happier than he had thought he could be. "How different the world," he wrote in his journal. "A few weeks ago and I wandered afield terrified by my loneliness in nature. . . . Now the whole earth is smiling, the sights and sounds of June never seemed so full and I can sit endlessly on hillsides and dream."

But the days in Salem were nearly over. In the late summer he and Bertha were engaged, and it became obvious that he would have to get another job before they could be married. Henry Turner Bailey, Dean of the Cleveland School of Art, liked Burchfield's work and had organized an exhibition of it at the school in 1917. Now he suggested that the young artist try wall paper designing, and he wrote to M. H. Birge and Sons of Buffalo, asking permission for Burchfield to submit some of his decorative 1917 watercolors. The firm was interested and asked him to come for an interview. He was given a job as assistant in the design department and reported for work the Monday after Thanksgiving, 1921.

III

BLACK IRON: 1921-1943

Here is the place for an artist—to dream a dream enveloped in misery—
to tell the truth about this is a poetic task.

—JOURNAL 1923

The first adjustment to Buffalo was hard. For six months Burchfield lived alone in rented rooms at 124 Whitney Place and 109 Mariner Street, suffering chronic homesickness. "Most terrible longings for my old life have assailed me tonight. I unpacked some of my old sketches, and they filled me with longing for the odd little events of a carefree country life—the record of a burning stump, a brook falling over a pile of stones in a hollow and huge buttonwoods lit up at sunset time." In January and again in March, 1922, he made weekend trips to Salem, where he was oppressed by the strangeness of his own room, which already seemed to belong to another person. He escaped to the Kenreichs' where there were card games and gaiety, a trip to the ice cream parlor, followed by an evening walk with Bertha in the woods. They stayed up till dawn. In February he wrote, asking her to set a date for their marriage. She suggested May, and on the 11th he took two small rooms at 170 Mariner Street—"my first home—their humble character seems fitting to me." They were married on the 20th.

Work at the wall paper factory, where Burchfield was eventually made head designer, was more demanding than the cost department at Mullins. Nine months of the year were spent in working out approximately one hundred new patterns with perhaps a dozen color schemes for each. Of these only a few, including several large "scenics," were by Burchfield himself, and today he feels that they are pure hack work and bear no relation whatever to his own painting. Three months went into "sampling the line," when it was Burchfield's responsibility to criticize the various color combinations and bring each into balance. He also had the difficult task of liaison between the office and the printing plant, a field in which personality clashes were frequent. "I modestly admit I did pretty well at it," he says in his autobiographical notes. "I translated their messages to each other into decent language, toned them down, or at times 'forgot' to deliver them. But it was a continual nagging nervous strain." The seven years that he worked for Birge were the least productive in his mature career.

At home, meanwhile, five children were being born at almost yearly intervals—Mary Alice (1923), Martha Elizabeth (1924), Sarah Ruth (1925), Catherine Esther (1926), Charles Arthur (1929). To Burchfield they were a deep fulfillment; still, they posed problems, the most immediate being one of space. Briefly the family took another apartment at 459 Franklin Street, but in April, 1925, they decided to move to the suburbs. Out the long flat stretch of Clinton Street, due east, just past the factories and sprawling food markets on the city's edge, they found the little village of Gardenville, which today melts imperceptibly into West Seneca, just as West Seneca melts into other towns that form an almost unbroken string of alternating stores, post offices and modest homes along the main highway. At 3574 Clinton Street, they bought a small, two-story, clapboard house set near the front of a narrow but deep plot, 33 by 450 feet. Surrounded by other houses and backyards on three sides, the front windows and pleasant porch of their home look across the highway toward relatively open country, cut by the steep banks of Buffalo Creek. There they have lived since 1925, adding, halfway down the backyard, a compact studio scarcely the size of a one-car garage. In these unpromising surroundings, all Burchfield's finest mature work has been done, and indeed the house and little yard, transformed in a hundred ways, have been the subject of much of it. "I don't believe there are many more banal and flat places than this village," he once wrote Edward Root, "and yet somehow after you live in a place for a certain length of time, things and places begin to belong to you." Periodically he planned to escape to a happier location, yet he liked to think of their narrow strip of land as "a little community...in which the lesser creatures and insects belong as much as we do," and sitting on the bench in front of his studio one morning, it seemed to him "that life could hold no greater peace and delight. This tiny corner of the earth that is ours gives a feeling of deep content and security; this is the base to which we can always come back and be ourselves, alone, completely free from the outside world. There is the sky above the village housetops, so vast and mysterious, full of the great loose sunlit, wind-slanted clouds that always come after a summer storm—through it I have access to infinity and down below, very tangible, is the yard and garden and how good all the things in it seem: the luxuriant tomato plants, now in sharp sunlight...the bed of vigorous cannae, the leaves struggling upward in whorled fashion; beyond them the onions with their crazy haphazard growth, and the orange day-lilies; on the right, in the shade of the pine trees, the confusion of the children's gardens with their predominating note of bouncing bet. It being Monday morning, into the garden, like the prow of a ship, juts a triangle of freshly washed clean-looking clothes, brilliant in the raw sunshine, cut by the slender shaft of the young birch tree with its lacy, drooping foliage.... At times the children pass through, intent on their play, seemingly unconscious of my presence; sometimes a wren sings, and there are the various sounds of village activities, all colored by the morning. The dull roar of motors passing on the street seems remote."

During these years, the Montross Gallery in New York handled Burchfield's work, gave him three one-man shows and sold a number of things, but not nearly enough to enable him to support a family. Meanwhile, his job at Birge's began to seem more and more of a drudgery. He would wake at night and relive "all the despised sensations of my daily work—the heavy, material, cocksure salesmen, the commonplace work that passes for art and the squabbles and colossal energy that must be put into it." He hated the commuting in crowded buses, the "neutral, non-seasonal" atmosphere of his office with its windows that looked on a cement courtyard enclosed by bare factory walls. By 1928, he had developed chronic indigestion, which the doctor warned him might turn into ulcers. Since three of his predecessors in the design department had died of cancer, it was not encouraging.

Early in 1928, word of Burchfield's discontent reached the Rehn Gallery, one of the best in New York, and Frank Rehn wrote, offering to take him on, but Burchfield hesitated. Then, in February, 1929, Edward Root, a collector and professor of art at Hamilton College, called on Burchfield to see his work. Root already owned several of his pictures and since the artist had nothing new to show him, he pulled out a portfolio of his 1916-17 papers. Root was enthusiastic, felt they should be shown in New York and at once arranged a meeting between Burchfield and Rehn at his home in Clinton, New York. Rehn assured the artist that he could sell enough work to support him, and Burchfield switched galleries, but in March he was still dubious about giving up his job. With four children and another on the way, it was a hard decision. "A spring of torture, despair and doubt," he wrote in his journal. "I have come to the end of things—a new life must commence." The deciding vote was cast by his wife. There was no question, she said, they must have faith in the future. On August 1, 1929, he quit work at the wall paper factory and was on his own.

"It is glorious to be away from the mill," he wrote to Mrs. Root that October. "Ideas are beginning to pile on me." Nevertheless, he found the adjustment harder than he had anticipated, and he later told Rehn that it was nearly two years before he got used to his independence. His hardest problem was the direction that his art should take. In Salem he had portrayed the mid-western village in all its aspects, and after he moved to Buffalo he continued to do so, both from observation and from recollection. But the city offered him a still wider range of subjects, its docks, bridges and railroad yards, its back streets and houses, which he began to paint soon after his arrival. As an interpreter of both rural and city life in his own narrow region, he had established himself, by 1929, as a pioneer in the regionalist movement which was then on the verge of becoming a dominant trend in American art. In a year Grant Wood would paint his famous *American Gothic,* and soon Thomas Craven would proclaim the Middle West as the true artistic center of America, and Benton, Wood and Curry its principal artists. What was Burchfield's true relation to this movement—would he identify himself with it or not?

On the whole, not, although there is no doubt that he was somewhat affected by its budding spirit. At various times in the 'thirties he expressed sentiments that were in general sympathy with the aims of the "American Scene" group. Listening to Sibelius' *Finlandia,* he wrote, "What a great thing it is for an artist to create something that is the epitome of the spirit of a whole nation. . . . Would that I could paint something that would bear the same relation to America." And once he reflected, "I would rather be a native of America than any other country I know, past or present." Yet it is significant that the regionalist note is never sounded by Burchfield and that he took an early dislike to its implications. "I notice of late that my name has not been used so much with the Benton-Wood-Curry idea," he wrote to Rehn in 1935. "If this is due to your efforts, a thousand thanks to you. . . . You would think that nothing original ever came out of America until youngsters in the middle-west started painting. I come out of the middle-west myself, but . . . I have a wholesome respect for the generation preceding me and . . . I don't want to appear to be scornful of or inimical to the so-called eastern artists. . . . There is no question of being eastern, western or whatnot!" His feeling, though he never quite resolved it in words, seems to have been that the artist should be faithful to those scenes that he knew and was moved to paint, but that no one milieu was inherently better than another. Perhaps this is regionalism of a kind, but certainly not of the militant sort that Craven promoted.

Furthermore, Burchfield's taste in art was extremely catholic and not at all affected by regionalist dogma. His enthusiasm for Edward Hopper's work is understandable in terms of his own aims, but he also admired Max Weber and thought him a very genuine artist, although

Deserted House.
1923.
Brush and India ink,
watercolor wash,
crayon, conté crayon,
lead pencil.
13¾ x 19⅞.
Collection of
Leona E. Prasse.

he could not understand Weber's subjects. He liked European masters as diverse as Vermeer, Rembrandt and Cézanne, while a 19th-century French painting exhibition at the Metropolitan Museum made him wonder, "Is this perhaps the greatest period in art to date?" Even these predilections were, one suspects, rather haphazard, depending largely on what exhibitions Burchfield happened to see, and they had no demonstrable effect on his own art. After a social dinner, someone once showed him a large stack of reproductions of paintings in a certain museum. "I was bored," Burchfield complained in his journal. "How is it possible to make people understand that artists are not interested in art?"

The paintings which Burchfield did of Buffalo in these twenty-two years were undertaken, then, in no regionalist spirit and under no strong exterior influences. His attitude toward the city was, in fact, a little ambiguous. For a brief period in the early 'twenties, it was tinged with social consciousness. "Pick out the raw elementary life to portray," he exhorted himself. "Life of the lake freighters—crude, harsh, and obscene. Life on the railroads. The life of rum-runners and auto bandits. Are you softening up? Get back to . . . fearless indictments of modern society and life." Actually, he undertook no such program— which was perhaps just as well—and this seems to have been one of the rare occasions on which he thought of himself briefly as the kind of social satirist that McBride had hailed in 1920 for his songs of hate. On the other hand, Burchfield was perennially interested in the people on the streets—particularly the odd and eccentric. Sitting on a trolley car, he would find himself staring at a strange man with rolling eyes, accompanied by a terrified looking woman with a heavy moustache, and a fat Negress; for hours they would haunt him as he tried to imagine their lives and what kind of a house they lived in. Going to work on the bus he thought, "Now is the moment. . . . Now is the time to live and do my best work—these people are the most interesting people on earth." He seldom painted them, except in a few pictures like *Promenade* and *Little Italy in Spring*, but something of his feeling for them went into his pictures of deserted streets and those inscrutable houses which continued to symbolize the lives they sheltered.

But Burchfield's dominant interest in the city was unquestionably the harsh beauty that he saw in it, where others found only ugliness, and the many moods that he sensed in it, varying with every change of season, weather and scene. By the harbor at dusk, the big grain elevators reflected in the black water seemed to have melancholy thoughts of their own. He would stand in the train yards, "drinking in through my eyes the soot-and-smoke-blackened surfaces, the coal-dust filmed earth, the gleaming rails," enjoying even the smell of the acrid, gray-violet smoke. Or he would walk uptown as night was falling just to get the feel of twilight settling over the city. He realized that these moods were subjective. "As I sat in an office on the fifth floor of a building downtown and looked out over the motley collection of buildings and noted the crude manufacturing shapes . . . I thought it is not what a place is that makes for art—it is what the artist feels about [it]." For him, Buffalo had beauty and a presence.

These two qualities alternate about evenly in the paintings which Burchfield did of the city. Not that they can be entirely separated; nevertheless, one group of pictures seems to reflect a predominantly esthetic pleasure in the shapes and textures of the industrial scene, whereas the other is more concerned with its romantic moods. In the first group are such watercolors as *Rainy Night* (1930), *Ice Glare* (1933), *Freight Cars Under a Bridge* (1933), *Black Iron* (1935), *Old Houses in Winter* (1941), *Iron Bridge and Winter Sun* (1943). These were subjects that moved him visually; he wrote that the spaces between freight cars had a special beauty, and he obviously delighted in the rugged pattern of bridge girders, the play of light on wet or icy pavements, the rich surfaces of unpainted clapboard houses. He spared no pains to record them as accurately as possible; painting *Black Iron*, he worked with such intensity that he sank into the boggy ground over the tops of his shoes and had to be rescued by a passing railroad worker. They are his most realistic paintings.

The other group, primarily concerned with mood, include *House of Mystery* (1924), *Sulphurous Evening* (1929), *The Parade* (1934), *Six O'Clock* (1936), *End of the Day* (1938), *House Corner in Spring* (1942). From the dates, it is apparent that these alternated with the paintings in the first group, except for *House of Mystery* and *Sulphurous Evening*, which are earlier and, as might be expected, more obviously romantic, harking back to the Salem houses with eyes and sinister personalities. Later, the moods became subtler, less melodramatic.

The "depressive chill" that a Communist parade gave him is remarkably suggested by the heavy arches through which it is seen. The sense of human weariness in *End of the Day* and of human warmth in *Six O'Clock* are achieved not only by the settings but by the light, the color, the very quality of the drawing; they pervade every inch of the paper. Many of these pictures are not "actual" scenes. They are composites, made up of studies done in various places, altered and recombined to create the feeling sought. Writing to Rehn of a related oil, *November Evening*, Burchfield described this process at its most difficult. "I have tried to express the coming of winter over the middle-west as it must have felt to the pioneers—great black clouds sweep out of the west at twilight as if to overwhelm not only the pitiful attempt at a town, but also the earth itself." This was the mood he wanted; its realization was complicated by the fact that the subject was principally imaginary, "based on fragmentary studies and memories." For months he worked by trial and error, "now adding, now destroying. . . . At one time I felt that my use of false fronts amounted almost to an obsession or mannerism. . . . And yet it was unavoidable, as I see it, and I hope I have handled the design in such a way that no other shapes . . . would be possible to create a unity." By which, he meant, of course, a unity both of design and of feeling.

As these pictures of city, town and village were exhibited, Burchfield's growing reputation had a tendency to become linked exclusively with such themes. "It has always been a bit annoying," he wrote Rehn, "that many of the critics and the public always think of me as the painter of the tumble-down street or the abandoned house," and he rejected the idea that there was "a special Burchfield subject." While there can be no doubt that his urban scenes were his most impressive work during this period, he was actually painting nearly as much in the country, moved by unpredictable impulses which would send him abruptly off to back roads and fields again. When such an impulse came, he would pack his sketching kit and a lunch, take the bus to Buffalo, then a local train to some outlying village. One bright September morning in 1929 he found himself, by this means, in Springville.

"I can think of no day for years that has been as perfect for me as was today, when I was so completely in accord with the world," he wrote in his journal. "Every ordinary stick and stone, every fence post,

shed, bush and tree was fully of interest—it seemed as though this was
the first walk I had ever taken—like the first created man coming into
a new land. . . .

"The town seemed full of glamour. I bought bananas at a grocery—
the sales lady and other customers seemed unreal to me. The street
that I took north was lined with huge elms and maples—soon I was in
the open country. The rich odors of September, probably intensified
by the heavy shower, delighted me—it was a combination of asters,
goldenrod, rotting wood, various flowers—cows in pastures added in-

Spring Evening.
1929.
Carbon pencil.
12½ x 17.
Collection of
the artist.

terest to the odor. I presently came to a little grove by the side of the
road and decided to walk through it.

"Entering it was like coming into a newly made woods on the first
day. I stood still, hardly daring to breathe. The thinning trees let sunshine through in freckled patches—the ground was lightly coated with
fresh brown leaves. . . .

"I pushed on up the hill road, knocking wild apples—their sharp
flavor a delight. The road attains the first plateau—a few clouds have
appeared in fleets along the southern horizon. A pasture wood stings
my curiosity. I enter it—an old cow-shed delights me as much as when
I am a boy. I found what seemed like a bird nest inside under the

eaves. As I touched it, a reddish brown mouse with a white belly ran out.

"The woods had evidently been struck by a near-tornado this summer as uprooted trees were scattered about in the greatest confusion. Crows were around. I sat on a fallen tree loath to leave the spot.

"Shortly beyond here . . . was a little bank covered with long dry grass and planted with what I can only call road-side maples. Such places seem to me to so inevitably belong to late summer that I decided to eat my lunch here. On the other side of the road were countless goldenrod—to the south, over a pasture, I could see the blue hills south of Springville.

"Shortly after continuing on my way, I came to a . . . road . . . along the top of a wide rolling hill—to the east lay a wide valley and beyond it another wide rolling hill-back and other hills. In the afternoon sunlight I went along singing and whistling idiotic songs. . . .

"Came upon an old farm-house that was a delight—a fine colonial shape, in a terrible state of repair—in front of it a huge black walnut tree. I made a sketch of it. First one of the occupants and then another come up to see what I am doing. . . .

"A heavy shadow suddenly fell across the battered house, and I turned to see that a wonderful formation of huge clouds had spread over the western sky, and then followed my only regret of the day— for all day I had let impressions come in so fully and had sketched so much that now I was not emotionally or physically up to drawing these clouds. As they came up, one behind the other, over the hill, they seemed to strike me with great power . . . a galaxy of shapes and colors so marvelous as to put despair into my heart. . . .

"I walked along torn apart by regrets on the one hand and feelings of awe and wonder and delight on the other. Presently a young farmer came along with a machine and took me to Boston . . . [where] I learned I could get a bus to Buffalo in an hour."

Every year there were such trips, for Burchfield's attachment to nature deepened throughout his life. It was a love that embraced many things. Weeds seemed as precious as fine flowers, a dandelion more beautiful than an orchid. Sketching one day in a swamp, he had to drop his brush a dozen times to watch the minute life in a pool—the caddice worms with their thatched houses, the leisurely water beetles, the "pipers" with their swelling bubbles—and he once refused to disturb a spider who had built a web from his desk-table to the light cord. He loved sunlight and he loved rain, when "the whole earth seems about to dissolve and blend upward into the mist, and a thousand odors are released and sent abroad." All seasons had their beauty, though his deepest feelings were for two months—March with its "vibrating, electric" quality and August with its powerful sun, its mysterious and terrifying nights. Every aspect had its mood. The song of frogs evoked the "deep, sullen mystery of spring." Crows were always associated with North; he had several of them stuffed and mounted in his studio where they frightened the cat but gave an atmosphere that he loved. There were magical spots in the woods, each with its own personality; in these he hesitated to stay too long, fearing to outwear the spell they cast.

Above all, nature became to Burchfield a refuge, a source of peace, a deeply religious experience. Painting beneath a broiling sun, the sweat pouring down face and arms, pestered by stinging flies, he would suddenly have the sense of a divine moment and his heart would sing for joy. Sometimes he would feel impelled to embrace the earth and would throw himself down on a hillside, the hot sun beating on his back, his face to the warm earth, while a great happiness came over him. Crossing the swamp barrens on a March day, he experienced without warning "one of those rare moments when time seems to stop and all seems at perfect peace and harmony between my Creator and myself. I had longed for scenes of the past, and I had longed for strange new scenes, but here in this humble spot eternity could be glimpsed." In a letter to Rehn, he rejected pantheism—"God is *in* His creation but separate from it"—in fact, however, he came very close to it.

Burchfield's attitude toward nature affected his life in many other spheres. He read with sympathy John Muir's account of his thousand-mile walk to the Gulf, he was delighted with Olive Schreiner's *Story of an African Farm*, and he copied many quotations from *Moby Dick* into his journal. More important was the intense and abiding admiration which he conceived for the music of Sibelius, "the greatest of living composers," he wrote the Roots. "I guess his appeal to me comes from the fact that he depicts nature almost exclusively . . . the shriek of the blizzard and biting cold . . . and waste desolation." Perhaps only Beethoven, of the great masters, stood higher in his affections, and for somewhat similar reasons. Not that his music was so plainly related to nature, but that it had in even greater measure a large, rugged, affirmative character and a deep romanticism. He liked particularly the late quartets, and he felt that hearing the Ninth Symphony was akin to religious experience. Soon after he was married, Burchfield began to collect records and to attend every concert that was given in Buffalo, as he has done since. Indeed, music has been one of the deepest pleasures of his life and, among the arts, has probably given him greater comfort and pure joy than painting, which has so often been a torture.

To say that painting has been a torture is no rhetoric. Aside from its creative problems, wracking enough at times, it is a lonely art, and Burchfield, a naturally lonely man, has suffered from a spiritual isolation that even the warmth of his family life could not entirely dispel. There were occasions when "the realization of my utter loneliness and its uncompromising necessity swept over me, almost crushing me with despair." Then he would think of the deaf Beethoven, reflect that greatness in art was in almost direct proportion to the aloneness of the artist, and thus come to a certain acceptance of the fact "that crowds and companionship are not for me." Nevertheless, he continued to suffer from his own deep reserve and inability to cross the barrier between himself and others. Showing his paintings to casual visitors in the studio seemed to him like undressing in public, yet he seldom had the courage to turn them away. An after-dinner speech that he had to give while jurying in Pittsburgh was pure agony; he was so nervous beforehand that he found it impossible to get into his tuxedo and had to change back into his business suit. Sometimes he thought that his years at the Mullins Company, when he never dared mention music or art, had fastened this habit of reticence on him; he knew that many resented it, but when he tried to overcome it he would have a sudden sense that he was going too far in the other direction and would retreat to reticence again. After thirteen years in Gardenville, he wrote Rehn, "I have few close friends around here [and] . . . we have no social life," while four years later he reflected, "It is my habit to fear the making of acquaintance with new people, and probably if no one else ever made the first overtures, I would never meet anyone." He once took a "psychological questionnaire" and sent on the score to Rehn: "I am only 17% self-sufficient and 96% introverted. So that's the kind of guy I am!"

Burchfield had always been subject to sudden changes of mood, like those which occurred before and after his Army career, and they descended on him even more frequently after he left the wall paper factory and faced the uncertain future of an independent artist. "I go forth one day and come back brimming full—and another day I return empty handed, dejected and morose; there is no regulating the thing." Beauty, he thought, is so ephemeral; the moment of its apprehension always passes, leaving only the banality of life. His own creative moods would evaporate in the same way. One day he would be working with enthusiasm, another he would be caught in depression, held powerless by an overwhelming languor and aimlessness. Sometimes the mood was darker; "I haven't a single idea for painting and nothing seems worthwhile. . . . How to combat these black moods. Yet perversely I seem to want to steep myself more and more in them. It is soul destroying." No year went by that they did not descend in one form or another, sometimes terrifying him by lasting for months. Yet in the end they always passed, as unpredictably as they had come. The change might happen while he was listening to music or standing in the backyard or walking the streets. More often it occurred while he was wandering through the woods, as on one June day near Gowanda, not trying to paint but answering the call of a cardinal bird, rescuing an inch-worm, watching a chipmunk. Suddenly there would grow within him a sense "of such peace and happiness that I find it difficult to put down my impressions." He was ready to work again.

In his painting, regardless of subject, Burchfield remained remarkably free of exterior influences. He once told Rehn that "an artist does like to feel he belongs to the scheme of things, to be 'necessary' to the age he lives in," but he came closer to the truth when he wrote in his journal, "I like to think of myself—as an artist—as being in a nondescript swamp, alone, up to my knees in mire, painting the vital beauty I see there in my own way, not caring a damn about tradition or anyone's opinion." This was the most realist phase of his career and he was much less concerned with style than with technique. He admired the scientific drawing of a corn-borer, posted in the railroad station, for its "precise outlines and exact intimate details," and he spent a whole day observing a farmer plowing so that he could correct the pattern of furrows in one of his pictures. When he undertook an ambitious oil, like the *Old House by Creek,* he would divide it into passages—the sky, the chimney groups, the bridge area, the water, the bank in the foreground—and make dozens of pencil studies for each, sometimes totalling several hundred drawings.

But Burchfield never felt at home in the oil medium, though he struggled with it for years. "I'm going to turn out some good oils or die in the attempt," he wrote Rehn in 1930, and by sheer persistence he painted a few canvases that were truly successful. Usually, however, it was galling work that exhausted him physically and emotionally. In 1938, working on one of his largest oils, a painting of the grain elevators at the harbor, he wrote in his journal, "Creation is not pleasure but agony," and when the picture failed to live up to his expectations, he virtually abandoned the medium.

Watercolor was always his first choice, and it was here that he developed, almost unconsciously, the highly individual technique which varied with different subjects and moods but was essentially a system of heavy, overlapping strokes that create a general effect of breadth, ruggedness and solidity. It is as far removed as night and day from the sparkling washes and spontaneous feeling of traditional watercolor technique, and it gave the medium a seriousness and range more commonly associated with oil. Its possibilities were still further extended as Burchfield increased the size and scale of his pictures, bringing them up to 30 x 40 inches and eventually, by piecing the paper out, to even larger dimensions. He made watercolor, in short, a major vehicle of expression, capable of as much breadth and variety as any other medium and particularly adapted, as he himself noted while admiring a locomotive one day, to the "hard-boiled realism of such things." Like the difference, he added quite justly, between Beethoven and the classicists.

This technique was not, of course, developed for purely realist ends —it is too broad, too moody for that. Asked to classify himself in 1940, Burchfield decided that the best description was romantic realist, for he was consistently and deeply concerned with interpreting the essen-

tial character of his subjects and his own emotional response to them.
Sometimes this is clearly demonstrable. The haunted appearance of
the old Gothic house in *Lace Gables* echoes an experience that he had
as he was sketching it, when his imagination suddenly peopled it with
his mother and himself as a child; while he looked, it seemed to grow
darker, quieter, imbued with a fearful feeling of death and isolation.
But such "explanations" are hardly necessary, for the mood is always
clearly realized in the painting itself. Even two superficially similar
landscapes, like *The Open Road* and *Snow Remnants*, are entirely
different in atmosphere, the first exultant with its sweeping curves
and bold pattern, the other bleak, composed of heavy, disconnected
forms but bathed in the luminous, tender light of early spring. Radical
alterations of the actual scene were often necessary for such expressive
purposes, and Burchfield never hesitated to make them, although it
appears to have been a largely instinctive process. Returning once to
Steubenville, which was the subject of his *End of the Day*, he was
himself "amazed at how I had changed this scene, partly unconsciously"
—an experience that was repeated on other occasions.

It is difficult for one who is not an artist to realize the intensity of
Burchfield's continuing struggle to perfect his interpretive means.
When he travelled, he would paint things mentally, trying to imagine
how he would solve their problems. Periodically he would feel that
he did not yield enough to impulse, and there would follow a period of
spontaneous work, done directly from nature. "One of my greatest
faults," he once wrote Edward Root, "has been to depend almost
entirely on my studio work. . . . I got into a rut of using over and over
again certain conventions which, though they are of my own invention,
are just about worn threadbare. . . . I need to paint right in front of
the object, feel it, experience that emotional state that actual presence
produces in us." But then he would decide that spontaneity was not
enough, that he wanted to dream about his subjects and absorb their
essence fully before painting them. So he would return to the studio
and try working from sketches and drawings made some time before.
Or he would combine the two methods, start a painting outdoors and
put it aside, sometimes for years, allowing it to grow in his mind
before finishing it in the studio. He tried what he called "dummies"—
small studies in color to fix the idea, but gave them up since they

often destroyed his impulse to do the large picture. He tried, and
still uses occasionally, cartoons, or full size charcoal drawings of an
intended picture, in which the main problems of design are worked
out. The important thing, he told himself, is first to establish the mood,
then the painting will take care of itself; and indeed he could sometimes work with great ease and rapidity, solutions to every problem
coming so fast that he would go without food or eat in front of his
easel lest he break the spell. "If I were only able to work so always!"
More often the task of sustaining his creative urge was a conscious,
agonizing effort. "There comes a time always, in painting a picture,
when it becomes a prison; I long to get away from it, to be quit of it
forever; yet the only release . . . must come from carrying it through."
In extreme cases, he would start again and again on a difficult problem,
until "I finally reach a point when, in a rage, I destroy all I have done
so far—and at that moment, unknown to myself, I have solved it."

When Edward Hopper wrote his article on Burchfield for *The Arts*
in 1928, he made two perceptive observations. The first might have
applied to his own painting as well. "Is it not the province of work
such as Burchfield's," he wrote, "to render to us the sensations that
form, color, and design refuse to reveal when used too exclusively as
an aim in themselves, and which words fail to encompass?" That is the
realist or, more accurately, the romantic realist position in a nutshell.
He added that a distinctive element in Burchfield's style was "a certain
baroque treatment of perimeters," and this defines very well the more
romantic phase of Burchfield's middle period, a phase which stretched
from the Salem papers of late 1918 to the early 1930's. It is particularly
noticeable in the pointed, thrusting shadows of *House of Mystery*
(1924), the shimmering reflections and embroidered skyline of *Rainy
Night* (1930) and the ragged, drooping branch pattern of *Evening*
(1932). It recurred, though not often, in a few later pictures like
Lace Gables (1935). In their restless movement, their elaboration
of picturesque detail and general romanticism, these are all related
stylistically to such Salem work as *Black Houses* and *Noonday Heat*.

But in 1933, with *Ice Glare* and *Winter Bouquet*, Burchfield began
to move in a more sober direction. This was the year that he wrote to
Edward Root of his revulsion against his past work, his resolve to
work directly from nature. His forms now became simpler and in-

creasingly static. They were more realistic in the sense that he no longer decorated them with the lively embroidery of his earlier work, but they were also generalized to a greater degree, heavier, broader in treatment, more architecturally composed. The trend was intensified during the next few years in *The Parade* (1934), *Six O'Clock* (1936), *Old House by Creek* (1938), *Old Houses in Winter* (1941), *House Corner in Spring* (1942) and *Iron Bridge and Winter Sun* (1943). From about 1938 on, however, he tended to modify somewhat his extreme severity, returning, though never very far, toward the active designs of the preceding years—a fusion that can be seen in pictures like *End of the Day* (1938) and *Edge of Town* (1941). All of these paintings have their own romantic moods, but they are both more simply and more subtly stated than in the earlier work, and they cover a wider range.

The outward events in Burchfield's life after he left Birge and Sons were scarcely different from those of any American family in the suburb of a small industrial city. The children grew up, were educated, left home to take jobs or get married. In the summer of 1933, his sister Frances and his mother died within nine days of each other—a loss that went very deep. He was with his mother that last night. "At four o'clock as I sat holding her hand and wrist in which

Farm Landscape in July. 1943. Conté crayon. 10¾ x 17. Collection of the artist.

the pulse was steadily growing weaker, all the robins seemed to go mad with singing at the same moment; a little later a red-bird came and sang from a wire out front, clear and strong—" he could write no more.

He had his own troubles, too, one of the worst being a violent attack of lumbago that struck him "like the blow of a club" in 1930 and that recurred at intervals thereafter. It was doubtless caused in some measure by Burchfield's persistent habit of painting outdoors under the most improbable conditions—now huddled under his umbrella in a summer rainstorm, his legs streaming water but the paper protected; again working in snow squalls with his sponge and water freezing but thinking, "What unalloyed happiness.... The painting takes on a character it could not have under milder conditions." After he bought his first car in 1934—to take the muse riding, he explained to Root—he extended his outdoor operations, pushing into the Zoar Valley and on overnight trips as far as the desolate, poor country around Emporium (where the village prostitute tried to buy one of his sketches) and even into Pennsylvania. There he would abandon the car and trudge for miles through all kinds of country and weather. "You cannot experience a landscape until you have known all its discomforts," he thought. "You have to curse, fight mosquitoes, be slapped by stinging branches, fall over rocks and skin your knees, be stung by nettles, scratched by grasshopper grass and pricked by brambles ... before you have really experienced the world of nature." This he continued to do despite the ever-present threat of his lumbago.

Unlike most present-day artists, Burchfield refused to teach during these years and was totally dependent on sales for the support of his family. Rehn did remarkably well for him, holding one-man exhibitions of his work nearly every year from 1930 on. Gradually Burchfield's fame grew. The Museum of Modern Art showed his early watercolors in 1930. The Pennsylvania Academy presented him a prize in 1929, the Carnegie Institute in 1935, and many similar awards followed. John Rothenstein, director of the Tate Gallery in London, came out to the studio, proclaimed his hope of buying several early things, but never did. The Carnegie Institute gave him a retrospective exhibition of 63 paintings in 1938, an experience that terrified him in prospect but pleased him by its critical success. Thereafter, he found his services increasingly in demand as a juror for various important events, among them the World's Fair exhibition in 1939, the Artists for Victory in 1942, the fine arts jury of the Guggenheim Foundation from 1940 on.

Fame also brought him a number of commercial offers, some of which he accepted. The magazine *Fortune* sent him to Altoona and Harrisburg in 1936 to record the railroad yards; there he was caught in the disastrous flood of that spring and wrote Rehn, "When desolation is too much for a Burchfield, you know it's pretty bad." The following year the same magazine sent him to Texas to cover the making of sulphur and to West Virginia to paint the coal mines.

He rather enjoyed his experience in the mines where he was taken deep underground and had to work by the light on his cap. But *Fortune* did not reproduce the resulting sketch, claiming it was unsuitable for technical reasons, and the whole experience "turned out a little sour," as he wrote to Root. Perhaps the truth was that Burchfield never felt completely comfortable working on a commission; after so many years of independence, of choosing his own subjects and following his own timetable, it gave him the sensation of being put "on the spot," and he made no effort to seek further work of this kind.

Unfortunately, fame did not automatically guarantee sales, and there were many nights when Burchfield lay awake, worrying over the precarious state of their finances. Private collectors had a way of shying at the bleakness of his subjects, like the woman who cancelled her purchase of his *Shed in the Swamp* (now a part of *The Glory of Spring*) because her husband had had a hard youth farming in just such a region, and found the picture depressing. "Doggone him," Burchfield wrote Rehn, "no one ever plows in that kind of country, you wander through swamps for the sheer pleasure of it— at least I do." There was scarcely a year when they were not pinched severely at one time or another, and he often faced the real possibility that he might have to take a part-time job to make ends meet. There were moments when he longed to forget about money, to spend as the impulse came, even to run into debt. "One of the earmarks of a great artist," he thought, "is the capacity for large, generous living . . . even if it involves him in difficulties. Somehow he extricates himself and even lives on a grander scale." But by temperament he was utterly incapable of following such a program, so there would be another

Easter with no new clothes for anyone, the car used less for sketching and a letter to Rehn to see if any funds were due him.

The second World War brought additional problems. Sketching one day along the Buffalo Creek, Burchfield was stopped by a policeman who told him it was restricted territory and took his license number, name and address. That meant the end of industrial subjects, and soon gasoline rationing cut severely into his trips to the country. But it was his personal relation to war that preyed on Burchfield the most. He was too old for the Army, and his mind kept turning to the possibility of helping through his art. Yet he loathed the idea of portraying the physical conflict, and he told Rehn that he could not bring himself to paint songs of hate or pessimism, quite simply because he did not feel that way. The war frightened him with forces that were incomprehensible; "underneath it all is something tremendous and terrifying . . . and that is what I don't understand." So he turned his back to it in his work, feeling, as he wrote again to Rehn, that "the only worthwhile artist is one who can create detached works of art, regardless of the catastrophes that come, whether they are of the world or of his own personal life." It was not an easy decision, and many months passed before he achieved a degree of real detachment.

Detachment, indeed, is not a characteristic of the romantic artist, nor is it a quality that can be easily associated with Burchfield at any time in his career. This is nowhere more apparent than in his attitude toward youth, and especially toward his own youth in Salem, Ohio. "Youth," he thought, when he was still not quite thirty, "is a thing of the spirit . . . youth must be retained . . . the courage to experiment . . . and seeing life as a poem." As middle-age threatened him with its more relaxed attitudes, he fought against it with the valiance of true romanticism, while recurring visions of Salem overwhelmed him at intervals with an aching nostalgia. "I long for the old forgotten moods," he wrote in his journal, "—for endless summer days spent in the Ohio hills—for the July days of 1918 spent in the hill country south of Salem —for the old burning optimism—for the joy of God's newly created earth . . . for the old homely interest in common objects." It was not only the country that haunted him, but the crude life of Ohio's towns and villages, the recollection of "men going home on icy walks past hard buildings touched at their tops by the last glow of the fading day—cold dark windows—fried potatoes." He often re-read his own early journals, reflecting that they sounded like the writings of another person. "The rhapsodic utterings of that period, expressive of my pure unattached joy in a marvelous world, fill me now with unutterable sadness and longing—almost of terror. Could I but once again walk in those . . . meadows of wonder." Sounds and smells evoked without warning pictures of boyhood as vivid as Proust's. A factory whistle blew, and he saw a long, dusty road at noontime, flanked with fields of buttercups. The odor of pumpkin vines brought back an elusive memory of dried bean stalks which obsessed him for months because he could not place it exactly. Periodically he returned to Salem, and once he made a pilgrimage to Post's Woods that was "like digging open an old wound."

These feelings and sensations, which occurred throughout his middle years, were intimately connected with his art. In his early watercolors he sensed a magical, spontaneous quality that he felt had vanished from his mature work. Looking at them again was a disturbing experience, and he found himself wondering if "I have lost more than I have gained with the years. This is not really so I expect, nor should a healthy artist feel so." Yet they continued to occupy his mind and from the early 'thirties he began to be tempted at increasingly frequent intervals to see if he could return once more to that free, calligraphic manner, that imaginative response to nature. In 1931, as he was walking along the railroad tracks, he found himself thinking of a 1917 picture of two hollows, one still locked in winter, the other showing the first signs of spring. In 1919, he had tried to overpaint it in gouache, but had put it aside as a failure. Now he suddenly wondered if it could not be salvaged. Hurrying home, he spent the next few days painfully removing the gouache without harming the original painting below, and then made a few new changes in watercolor. The results did not live up to his expectations, and in 1933 he started to paint a much larger modern version of it, the *Two Ravines*, which was not finished until ten years later. His thought at this time was not to return to the manner of 1917, but rather to recapture the 1917 mood in terms of his present style. "As an artist grows older," he wrote to Mr. and Mrs. Root, "he has to fight disillusionment and learn to establish the same relation to nature as an adult as he had when a child—it will not be like it, but the ratio of the emotion will be the same. That is my struggle now."

In practice, however, this turned out to be impossible. The sober, predominantly realistic style of the 'thirties was simply not suited to express the romantic fantasies of youth. Gradually he began to realize this, though it was not until 1943 that he fully accepted the fact and acted on its implications. In the meantime the early papers exerted a steadily growing pull on his mind and his emotions. In 1939, Rehn decided to have another exhibition of them, and early in February Burchfield began remounting them. One was an incompleted sketch of the peter bird. Feeling that it should be put into a finished state, he went to work on it. "This led first to one and then another until I was soon so immersed in work that I could scarcely take time off to eat and often came out at night to mount sketches for the next day. I became so wrapt up in these ideas that I longed for the old days ... and in short to be a youth again." Months later his mind was still imprisoned by those early nature fantasies; "the things," he thought, "that I attempted then!"

Summer Storm. 1947. Conté crayon. 10⅞ x 16⅞.
Collection of the artist.

IV

THE INLANDER: 1943-1956

I will always be an inlander in spirit. The ocean ... does not lure
my imagination. Without discounting its awe-inspiring grandeur, it is not for
me, and surely it has a worthy rival in a hay or wheat field
on a bright windy day.

—JOURNAL 1954

It was April 19, 1943, and a cold rain was blowing in out of the east.
In the studio Burchfield was mounting some early Salem sketches pre-
paratory to finishing them, a job he had been doing on and off for the
past week. It not only sharpened his perceptions of nature, he was
thinking, but also made him see the world with a fresher, more inno-
cent eye. On the easel stood the huge, nearly finished watercolor *Two
Ravines*, painted with forceful realism. Beside it was the smaller, more
fanciful 1917 paper which had inspired it, the one that he had over-
painted in 1919 and had tried to restore in 1931. His mistake at that
time, he now realized as he stopped to study the picture, was the "tonal
painting" which he had added in an attempt to bring it up to date, stylistically speaking. "What it needs," he suddenly concluded, "is to be
restored completely to the 1917 manner." Furthermore, he would enlarge it by pasting strips of paper around the edges and "adding the
kind of elements I would have put in at that time, and in the same
manner." It would thus be partly a restoration, but it would also be
a new composition worked out in a conscious return to his early fantastic style. This required, he felt, fresh observation in the spirit and
mood of those earlier years. Two days later, he spent the afternoon in
a newly discovered ravine south and east of Boston, making endless
sketches. "The dark day, closed in by thick clouds that seemed almost
to touch the earth, gave the ravine a dim cave-like quality, rendering
every object mysterious, or even sinister. Everywhere I looked I saw
things to record—stumps, roots, stone ledges, a dim hollow with a black

pine group glowering against the sky on its upper edge, and once a large bird flew up from my feet and disappeared eerily under an overhanging hemlock branch.... I did not leave until six, when a fine drizzly rain began to fall."

The Coming of Spring, as this first reconstruction was finally called, marked a profound change in Burchfield's art. It released something in him, he wrote in his autobiographical notes, "a long pent-up subconscious yearning to do fanciful things, and once started, it seemed to sweep onward like a flooded stream; there was no stopping it." With mounting excitement, he turned to other subjects. Early in 1944, he enlarged one of his favorite 1918 papers, *The Song of the Peter Bird,* from 25½ x 20½ inches to 36 x 52 inches, thinking as he did so, "The longing to hear this bird again on . . . a brilliant day in March in the hollows is so strong at times as to make me ill." The new version took him six years before it was finally completed as *Sun and Rocks.* In the meantime, many other reconstructions were started, taking form in various ways.

"My reconstruction jobs of my early things has entered a new phase," he wrote to Rehn in 1944. "I am taking some that were not quite 'successes' (but which had a worthy aim in them) adding to them and adding or changing the elements to bring out to the full what I was aiming at.

"Then there are many things that never got beyond pencil studies, but some of them pretty complete. I want to carry them out on a grand scale, trying to preserve the 'early' romance, but doing them in my mature manner.

"Then there are some that I destroyed and want to try to resurrect. . . .

"Of course I can't bring but a few of these to completion in any one season, but I am laying the plans and starting them. The world is new to me again."

Later in 1944, he wrote to Rehn again, clarifying his convictions about his whole stylistic development.

"To me now, the 1920-1940 period (roughly speaking) has been a digression, a necessary one, but not truly in the main stream that I feel I am destined to travel. . . . During that middle period I was searching for an appreciation of form and solidity and a painting quality that the 1917 things lacked. Now, it seems to me, I am in danger of painting too realistically, and must try to recapture the first imaginative and romantic outlook, and even go beyond the scope of that period."

This, he explained, was difficult—hence the use of the early papers as a starting point. In enlarging them, "I aim to leave the original untouched as much as possible. . . . Even though I consider them as not quite successful for their period, I want to keep them as a record.

"I feel happier than I have felt for years," he concluded. "I'm going to give you more sounds and dreams, and—yes, I'm going to make people smell what I want them to, and with visual means."

Actually, it was impossible, as Burchfield knew, to turn the clock back twenty-six years and recapture without change the iconography and style of that distant time. What he had to do was to develop a parallel manner based on the same romantic attitude toward nature but incorporating to some extent his mature resources. He was quite conscious now, for instance, of futurist precedent when he employed the device of repeated shapes to denote movement, but his own application of it was somewhat different, particularly when he used it to represent waves of repeated sound in such pictures as *Autumnal Fantasy*. For the most part, he tried to build on his own earlier discoveries, extending them in new directions. Thus he revived, in subtly altered form, the abstract conventionalizations of mood that he had used in 1917, and worked out many new motifs to supplement them. His method was a combination of observation and invention. Working on a picture of grasshoppers, he would spend a day in the studio devising conventionalizations of the insects, then return to the field which was to be his setting in order to give life to the invented forms—a process which often gave rise to unpremeditated revisions and improvisations.

Stylistically, the reconstructions posed a problem that is nowhere mentioned by Burchfield but is quite apparent in the pictures themselves. He had long been used to working on a large scale, and he wanted to continue to do so. "I feel free and unhampered; it is as if I could better let the forces of nature control my brush." On the other hand, the early watercolors were almost all small, and the fanciful, calligraphic manner in which they were painted was essentially a small-picture technique. He was, therefore, faced with a dilemma. Either he must bring the original into scale with the enlarged paper by considerably repainting it (which he did not want to do), or he must keep it intact and fill in his new areas on a matching scale. At first, he generally chose to do the latter. In the case of *The Coming of Spring*, this was relatively easy because the enlargement was not great. But in certain big reconstructions which followed, like *The Sphinx and the Milky Way* or *Summer Afternoon,* the problem became acute and was not solved entirely successfully. Here Burchfield used a multitude of small strokes arranged in whorls, zig-zags, repeated undulations and similar patterns, then combined these to form the larger masses of foliage, sky, etc. The small strokes were apparently designed to serve a double purpose; they contributed a decorative or fanciful note of their own, and they acted as a kind of transition from the intimate scale of the original to the big one of the reconstruction—like the small bricks in a large house. The trouble is that they are so active, so varied, so full of character that they do not work inconspicuously like bricks, but give the surface a restless, intricate quality that is not always pleasant in pictures of such size. The effect was further marred in certain papers by Burchfield's return to the brighter colors of his early work. On the 1917 scale, these had a rich, jewel-like character; on the greatly expanded one of the reconstructions, they sometimes became either metallic or too sweet.

But these were transitional difficulties and were soon overcome. Perhaps the one factor that helped Burchfield most to solve them was that he continued, and has always continued, to paint directly from nature in a much more realistic vein. After finishing the highly stylized *Autumnal Fantasy,* he wrote Rehn, "I felt a violent urge to paint outdoors, and I did so, even though it was pouring rain (put a huge umbrella over me). . . . The result is just the sort of thing people expect from me, and incidentally I love it too. So there's not going to be any violent cleavage in my work." Now that he had put industrial subjects behind him, he gave himself wholly to nature—not only to her imaginative interpretation (which produced the fantasies), but also to a relation that was direct, unthinking, purely emotional. He would lie on a bed of dry leaves, looking up at the sky through the branches of a tree, feeling only a beauty that was "almost too great to be borne." Or he would stop for a moment in a meadow just to savor its rich smells and infinite variety, thinking that it was like the very smile of nature herself. He played games with her; one was called "sun-images"—you glanced at the sun, then away, seeing its image superimposed on the landscape; another was to lie for a time with your eyes closed—when you sat up suddenly and opened them, the whole earth would quiver briefly with a white trembling light. There was even something of the scientist, or at least the naturalist, in this relation. He found Audubon's *Journals* deeply sympathetic, and in his own he took to recording the first hepatica, the first redbird, the first cicada of every season. He kept a wildflower garden in the backyard, as he had when a boy, dug plants for it on many of his sketching trips and dreamed of becoming a hybridizer and developing a red hepatica.

This direct relation with nature found expression in a series of small watercolors—*Goldenrod in December, July Clouds, Pear Tree in September*—which Burchfield did at the same time as the fantasies. Despite his letter to Rehn, they are not much like his nature painting of the middle years, being much freer and imbued with a quality that fairly sings. The color is more varied, ranging from the rich blue and gold harmonies of summer to the pale grays and browns of winter. While they are primarily realistic in intention, the new freedom which his fantasies gave him is reflected in certain passages of patterned branches and foliage, which are almost abstract. These are like vivid accents integrated in the whole scheme, and they give the pictures a new measure of vitality. Burchfield even used the same lyrical style in a few larger papers, of which the most impressive is *The Three Trees*, bought by Miss Alice MacMillan for the Salem, Ohio, library as a memorial to the family bookshop that her father had founded and as a testimonial to Burchfield's mother, whose classmate she had been. Into this three-by-five-foot watercolor the artist put all one side of his feeling for Salem—not its night-haunted moods or bleak industrialism, but rather its idyllic land-of-youth quality. Appropriately, he turned for this purpose to the free bravura of his new realism, building the trees into massive towers against the flat landscape, adding a dramatic note in the long streamers of sunlight, but essentially preserving his own exact memory of a deeply loved scene.

Yet for Burchfield, this was never enough. Nature had too many moods, and his own romantic response to them was too ardent to be imparted by even the freest kind of realism. A thunderstorm still gave him "all the thrill of 1915," and he wondered despairingly if he would ever be able to paint its full glory and mystery. The cawing of crows had a savagery that was spine-chilling. Even the little backyard at Gardenville, always beautiful, took on at times a strangely altered character. Airing the dog there one moonlight night, it suddenly seemed to him that the familiar scene was transformed in a way that defied description. "It assumed an aspect of remote, primitive char- acter—much more vast than our village site actually is, as though I were standing near the edge of a rude plateau and beyond that reced- ing line of poplar trees was a limitless expanse of moonlit lowlands." Many of these moods were still bound up with nostalgia for his Salem youth. He longed to break the confinement of adulthood, "to come up the Painter road, barefoot, hot, tired, hungry and thirsty—and to feel the almost terrifying power of the Summer Solstice noon beating down on the white, dusty road." He was haunted by memories of twilight in the Ohio woods, of hepaticas blooming before the dark cavern of a hollow tree. Periodically, he returned to Salem, with widely varying results. On a trip in 1943, it seemed a nightmare town, dead, empty, incredibly dingy, with no relation to the village he remembered. Two years later he took his wife, showed her his favorite spots in the woods, did a little sketching and was supremely happy. "Very little was changed, except for the better." In another two years, he was back again in a more elegiac mood. Walking through the rooms of Aunt Em's house, full of family associations, he thought that this too would soon be gone and only memories remain.

All these factors, so much more complex in life than on paper, en- tered into his art. He was impelled toward fantasy and the evocation of mood, yet realism was inadequate for this purpose, and the recon- structions involved serious esthetic problems. The only true solution could be a new style that made use of all his great technical skill, that was appropriate to the big scale which he preferred and yet revived and carried forward the fantastic elements of 1917. As early as 1944 Burchfield realized this when he wrote to Rehn, "I want to conven- tionalize a mood or motive from nature and then do it in a free calli- graphic manner, plus what I have learned about form and weight since." Turning now to original compositions, which were no longer tied to the small forms of his early watercolors, he began to experiment with big, semi-abstract shapes that spread over large areas of the sur-

Sun and Cobwebs.
1949.
Pen and India ink.
11 x 17⅛.
Collection of
William Matthewson
Milliken.

face. In *Midsummer Caprice*, striving to express the weirdness of the insect world, he devised a writhing form that fills the sky and flows over much of the landscape—a symbol that is less specific but more mysterious and suggestive than the little V-lines used to denote insect song in 1917. When he now undertook the evocation of sound, as in *Clatter of Crows in Spring Woods, Song of the Marsh* and many other pictures, he continued to work with larger symbols which are more abstract and seem to saturate the entire painting with the effect sought. He was perhaps most successful when he wove these into natural forms instead of superimposing them on the surface. Thus in *Hush Before the Storm*, where he was aiming at "something dark and mysterious, like a solemn Bach fugue," he used the branches themselves in a repeated Gothic-arch pattern. Sometimes he worried lest he had pushed fantasy too far, and there are indeed a few pictures which seem a little forced in this respect. But on the whole, the new symbolism was both more powerful and more truly visual than that of his early years.

Most of these watercolors were also painted with greater breadth and freedom than either the early work or the first reconstructions, for Burchfield soon discovered that the flat, calligraphic handling of his youth was too limiting. He tried it briefly in *Midsummer Caprice* and one or two other pictures, but quickly abandoned it in favor of the full range of tonal effects and the deep space of his mature realism.

His abstract symbols, themselves, became three-dimensional; the strange sky-form in *Clatter of Crows,* for instance, is woven through the whole design, advancing from the far background nearly to the frontal plane of the picture. Soon the same painterly handling began to find its way even into the reconstructions, for not all of these were tied as closely to their 1917 originals as those discussed above. Many of them grew out of unfinished work, some even from pencil sketches. In these, the early "core" had to be largely repainted anyway, and he was therefore freer to treat them in the new manner. Often the original became nearly lost in this process, and the whole concept changed radically as the painting progressed. One of his finest pictures, the big *Sun and Rocks* of 1950, grew in this way. It started with the 1918 *Song of the Peter Bird,* but the bird and his voice are perhaps the least important elements in the finished paper. It owes its main character to a day in 1948 when he went sketching in "Rock City," a fantastic hillside covered with jumbled boulders and honeycombed with caves. Returning to the studio, "I played the Sibelius Fourth Symphony—the impressions of the rocks and the music intermingled, each magnifying the other, and presently I had a vivid inner-eye picture of a strange fantastic scene in some unknown Northland. . . . I felt in fine fettle, able to tear into the picture, making changes and inventing new themes and details. I put into the sun all the devastating, destroying power of that 'star' that I feel on a March sap day." With so much independence, it mattered little whether the picture was a reconstruction or not, for it is painted with all the solidity and vigor so patiently acquired in those long middle years, now perfectly fused with the fervor, the poetry and fantasy of Burchfield's youth. It is one of the most original romantic paintings of our day.

Burchfield's return to fantasy had, at first, a chilly reception from critics and collectors. One of the latter, who had already bought a number of his early works, called at the studio in 1945, looked at his *Autumnal Fantasy* and remarked, "People will ask if you cut off your ear after painting that." The artist had not held an exhibition at Rehn's since 1943, and that had included none of the new work. Now, in November, 1945, there was enough ready to make a show devoted entirely to the fantasies, and he sent them on to the gallery. Would Rehn like them or not? It meant a great deal to Burchfield, for he had come to depend on the veteran dealer's opinion to a greater extent than is common in such relations, partly, no doubt, because of the deep personal friendship that had developed between them. Whatever the cause, Burchfield often repainted or "corrected" whole sections of his pictures at Rehn's suggestion and relied heavily on his judgment. So it was a blow when, instead of the usual enthusiastic letter, a very dubious note arrived saying that it might not be possible to hold an exhibition during the present season. It cast Burchfield into a profound gloom, and only his wife's unbounded faith, he wrote in his journal, gave him the courage to continue in his new direction. Then, for a time, the prospect brightened. In mid-December, Rehn wrote again to say that he personally liked the work and had hesitated only because of the adverse reaction of several critics and "certain museum people." Since then, he had been showing the paintings to many of his artists, and they were all enthusiastic. The exhibition would be held at once, in January. When it took place and the reviews began to appear, some critical doubts were indeed expressed, but *The Blizzard* was on the cover of *Art Digest*, and the accompanying article by Jo Gibbs was warmly sympathetic. Nevertheless, Burchfield remained apprehensive for some time at the general lack of understanding. "I have been in a sort of blue funk about exhibiting my work," he wrote Rehn in 1947. "Since I started on this new project, the interest in it has unquestionably declined. . . . I suppose the only thing to do is to keep hammering at the public indifference. But sometimes at four o'clock in the morning, courage wanes."

Well it might, for sales slumped badly after the 1946 show. This was doubly discouraging because they had started to revive after the early war years; now, just when the future began to look more secure, the old nagging worry about finances had to be faced all over again. In 1946 he had to borrow from Rehn. In 1948 funds were dangerously low, but he was saved later that year when the Munson-Williams-Proctor Art Institute bought his *Sphinx and the Milky Way*. In 1952 his finances were again precarious. Hoping to attract more modest collectors, he took to making small replicas of his large papers, often with variations—an experiment that was only partially successful. He kept his old car until it had gone 110,000 miles; it was still running, he

wrote Rehn, but "the grasshoppers have chewed up the fenders quite
a bit." If the industrial subjects of his middle years had offended by
their drabness, the new work seemed equally offensive for other reasons. "The great difficulty of my whole career as a painter," he reflected
in a moment of depression, "is that what I love most . . . not only holds
little of interest for most people, but in many of its phases is down-
right disagreeable, and not even to be mentioned! I love the approach
of winter, the retreat of winter, the change from snow to rain and vice-
versa; the decay of vegetation and the resurgence of plant life in the
spring. These to me are exciting and beautiful, an endless panorama
of beauty and drama, but . . . the mass of humanity remains either
bored and indifferent or actually hostile. And so I sit among my pictures, neglected, like them, by the buying public. There seems no solution."

But these were the low moments. Between them came many encouraging signs of Burchfield's growing reputation. Early in 1944 the University of Buffalo awarded him its highest honor, the Chancellor's Medal,
"in recognition of the fact that through his convincing revelation of
the beauty latent in familiar surroundings he has attained eminence
among the painters of his generation and has dignified Buffalo in the
eyes of the world." In April of the same year, the Albright Art Gallery
in Buffalo opened a retrospective exhibition of eighty of his paintings,
which did not, however, include any of the new fantasies. Nevertheless,
it was a gratifying experience. "I used to dread the idea of a retrospective," Burchfield wrote Rehn, "but no more. I just like to see my moods
again." And he added facetiously, "Gosh I just love me. I love to bask
in his glory—Burchfield's I mean. Bong! He's out, senseless." He, himself, was elected to the Board of Directors of the Albright Gallery in
1948. In 1944, Kenyon College offered him an honorary degree, and
the family took to calling him "Dr. Burchfield," though the joke wore
thin when Harvard, Hamilton College and Valparaiso University all
followed suit in the next few years. Perhaps the oddest indication of
his fame was the effusive letter he received in 1951 from a minor in-
come tax official in India begging for his autograph and assuring him
that he was indeed the greatest painter of this century. And the least
satisfactory honor, as things turned out, was his election to the National
Academy of Design in 1944. What happened next he explained in a

letter to Rehn: "I had to present the Academy with an oil portrait, 30 x 25, of myself. Now did you ever hear of anything so outlandish?" (He was, of course, neither an oil nor a portrait painter.) "I told them I didn't see how I could fulfill it, and they said, O. K. you're out. So that's that, but it leaves a bad taste and seems unnecessary."

Burchfield's reputation continued to involve him in a number of national art activities. He served on several American Academy in Rome juries and was twice offered the post of artist-in-residence there,

The Great Drought Sun. 1953.
Pen and brush with brown and India ink; black, sepia, and sanguine conté crayon; crayon; watercolor wash. 15⅛ x 19⅞. Cleveland Museum of Art, Norman O. Stone and Ella A. Stone Memorial Fund.

but refused. (He has never been abroad and has shown no strong desire to go.) He also served on the conservative panel of the Metropolitan Museum's contemporary watercolor exhibition jury in 1952 and, when the double-panel system was attacked, wrote a letter to the *Art Digest* defending it. Commercial and semi-commercial offers continued to come his way, but now he accepted only those which permitted him to work in his own fashion and turned down others which threatened to interfere with his serious painting. Thus he declined an invitation from Henry Varnum Poor in 1943 to join a group of war-correspondent artists headed for Alaska, although the money and his long-felt yearning to visit northern lands were a twin temptation. On the other hand, he designed several Christmas cards for Samuel Golden, painted a picture for the Chesapeake and Ohio Railroad because they told him he could choose any subject within their wide territory, and once he even did a Johnny Walker whiskey advertisement. His strangest commission came from the undertaker in Salem, Ohio, who ordered a "calm and peaceful" painting for his funeral parlor.

The old loneliness and sense of isolation have abated somewhat in Burchfield's later years, but they have never entirely left him. Standing in the darkening gloom of a wood at twilight, he is still capable of being overwhelmed by the sudden feeling that he is utterly alone, captive to a solitude both unendurable and necessary, "a prisoner who loved and hated his isolation." But such entries in the recent journals are much fewer. Similarly, the shyness which was once such agony has begun to wear off, though he still has difficulty in coping with suspicious farmers, like the one who found him painting on his land in a snowstorm and came roaring out at him, shouting, "What the hell's going on down here?" And he has never discovered the answer to kibitzers, who utterly paralyze his ability to paint. "I am always between two fires when such people seek to take advantage of me," he wrote recently. "If I am rude I regret it and if I am polite I am run over. Mostly I am polite and so let myself in for all sorts of annoyance and boredom." Such as the lady from Florida, whose husband was an amateur painter and who stopped her car one day to watch Burchfield sketching near the roadside. "Why that's pretty good," she said. "Is this professional work . . . ? Well, my husband's going to be greatly encouraged when I tell him about this." On the other hand, he has come to take a limited pleasure in events that would have been torture earlier; he enjoyed the award of the Chancellor's Medal at the University even though he had to be prodded into the receiving line and then shook a woman's hand so hard that she protested. And he can see the humor in some of the situations that his shyness and his absentmindedness create, such as the time he summoned a garage mechanic because his car refused to go, and was told that the only thing wrong with it was that he had forgotten to release the hand brake.

In Gardenville, the tight-knit family has gradually been dispersed.

By 1946 Martha was engaged and Sally, already married, had presented him with his first grandchild. "Don't feel any older," he wrote Rehn, although "I have all the earmarks of a grandfather—thinning hair—swelled head—graying temples—protruding chest, etc.—all except the gout and I'm not wealthy enough for that." By 1947, Mary Alice and Cathy had left home to take jobs in other cities, and when Arthur entered the Air Force the next year, their last child was gone. But there remained much—the comfort in work, the comfort in nature, the comfort in a marriage that is one of the rarely happy ones in the annals of successful artists, and the growing comfort in religion. For in 1944, after a spiritual struggle that lasted many years, Burchfield was formally received into the Lutheran Church, of which his wife had always been a member. It was a long road to travel for the young Salem painter who had despised all organized religion. Yet at heart Burchfield was always deeply religious, and no true understanding of his art can ignore this simple fact. He had early come to the belief that "true greatness, of the mountain peak variety, cannot be achieved unless the artist believes in, loves, fears and worships his Creator." But he had approached God through nature, not through the church. Once before, in 1936, he had nearly been converted but at the last moment had drawn back. On that occasion, "as I walked out through the backyard after supper and saw the clear sunset sky flecked with golden yellow clouds and saw the 'look' on the sunlit side of the shed, I realized that for me the only divine reality is the unspeakable beauty of the world as it is." Faith in the letter of revealed religion was infinitely more difficult, but he finally came to accept it. The old doubts vanished, though something of the painter and perhaps even the pantheist remained as he lay in bed one night listening to the rain on the roof and "thinking, as I often do of late, about Heaven and its character. It is impossible for me to imagine anything better or more beautiful than this world. . . . Like Corot, I hope there will be painting there, but somehow it does not seem logical."

With the children gone, there was more time and the Burchfields were freer in their movements. These factors, combined with financial pressure, led the artist finally to overcome his long aversion to teaching. It happened in 1949, but not without a struggle. Just the year before he had turned down a teaching offer and, writing to Rehn about it, had concluded, "Pardon my shudders." Now, when the University of Minnesota at Duluth invited him to take a class at a new summer session that they were inaugurating, he refused automatically, even though the terms were liberal. Finally the head of the Fine Arts College telephoned him to make a personal plea; there was something about the urgency of his voice, Burchfield says, that won him over, and he consented. On the whole, it was a pleasant experience, the one really bad moment being the demonstration that he found he was expected to give at the end of the course. For one who had never been able to paint in the presence of even his family, this loomed as "one of the worst ordeals of my career," but he got through it somehow. Home in September, the Duluth episode began to seem like a dream, not unpleasant but time lost forever from painting.

The ice was broken, however, and between 1950 and 1953 Burchfield taught a variety of summer and winter classes at the Buffalo Fine Arts Academy, the Art Institute of Buffalo, the University of Buffalo and at Ohio University in Athens, Ohio. Some of the groups were talented and responsive, others the opposite. There were entertaining incidents like that of the female student who had hysterics when cows were driven into a barn where they were sketching. Nothing that Burchfield could say of their harmless nature would reassure her, but she had her revenge a little later when a young bull chased him and

Fallen Tree.
1944/54.
India ink,
watercolor wash,
conté crayon.
11 x 17.
Frank K. M. Rehn
Galleries.

some other students up a bank. Perhaps the gayest group was the one at Athens in the summer of 1953, which said goodbye to him with its own Burchfield cheer: "Burnt sienna, raw sienna, yellow, ochre, blue —Burchfield, Burchfield, we're for you." But at best he was always a reluctant teacher, and there were times when the difficulties and the drudgery seemed unbearable. "I wish I had the courage to call the whole thing off," he once wrote in his journal. "It seems I have reached my limit of teaching incompetents." Some of his artist friends told him he took the job over-seriously, but he had too strong a sense of a good teacher's mission to follow their advice. The real trouble was that he could not give himself wholly to teaching at the expense of his work and suffered from the continuous conflict of demands.

And the demands of his serious painting, emotional and creative, were still heavy. In 1943 he told Rehn that he thought he had reached a more philosophical acceptance of those inexplicable moods that made work so difficult, but for many years they continued. Without warning, they would descend like a heavy veil between him and his art, bringing with them "an almost terrifying cessation of the painting impulse." At night he would lie sleepless, wracked by self-doubt. Each day he would think, "I must go out painting, but each day I do not want to go. What is the matter with me?" Even nature seemed to conspire against him at such times. Once, in sheer desperation he decided to paint the pear tree in a neighbor's backyard and put into it all the mood of the day and his own tortured spirit. At the moment he set up his easel, it began to rain. "I have just gone through a period of about the worst blues in regard to my painting I ever had," he wrote Rehn on another occasion. "Absolutely sunk. I not only doubted the value of the things I have been doing, but my worth as an artist, and wondered if I wanted to paint again."

His wife once told him she felt like shaking him, but these moods had to be lived out to their end. Sometimes he overcame them by sheer persistence, painting even when he knew that what he was doing would probably have to be scrapped. Sometimes they simply evaporated. Sometimes they ended in an apparently trivial incident; on a night walk, "the shadow of a porch falling aslant the face of a house gave me a peculiar thrill—I am ready to paint, I thought." Then, in recompense, would come the creative days when he felt a wonderful freedom to let himself go, experiment, improvise, surrender to the mood of the moment. "Ideas, memories and sensations are pouring in upon me," coming so fast, he told Rehn, that "I feel as if I ought to have four hands and forty-eight hours." Returning once from a short trip and its enforced idleness, his mind seemed on fire with new ideas. "When I went to lock the studio up, I made five or six drawings in relation to the new picture I had started. But that was not the end. After I got into bed I had to get up again and again to jot down ideas. My hand seemed to work without any help from my mind. It was almost midnight before the tumult in my brain subsided." At such moments he was filled with an absolute faith that his major works still lay ahead of him, that he would have the time, the energy, the creative power to complete them. "God is good to me . . . far beyond my deserts."

Something of that calmer confidence has entered into Burchfield's work during the last five or six years. It is as if the conflicting forces which had impelled him in different directions—now toward realism, now toward fantasy; now toward nature, now toward the works of man —had become more reconciled, more united in a single channel. For one thing, the acute nostalgia for his youth began to dwindle; he could return to Salem, as he did in 1948 and 1954, with scarcely a pang, and the journals no longer record those sudden waves of grief at a lost innocence and wonder. For a short time, he continued to enlarge some 1917 papers, but he treated them more freely, as he had in *Sun and Rocks,* and in 1954 he decided to give up entirely the large reconstructions, though he thought he might still finish early work which was incomplete, on its own scale. More and more, however, Burchfield has sought to express his mature moods rather than those of a vanished past. Sometimes these moods stretch all the way back to childhood, like his constant feeling for the mystery of North, but in such cases they have grown and matured with him, if one can say that of a mood, and have changed, sometimes subtly, sometimes radically, in their meaning. To the child, North was the magnetic terror of the dark and the unknown; it was black, and it was evil. To the artist in 1952, while it kept traces of its original character, it came to symbolize rather the elemental—"a thing I am always aiming at and hoping to achieve."

With his change of attitude, Burchfield's method of work has changed also. Increasingly, he has tended to decide first on the mood, then search in nature for a vehicle to express it. Sometimes the two processes happen almost simultaneously. While he was painting one day on an August landscape, the weather changed suddenly, big clouds came up, and a feeling of autumn replaced that of summer. Abandoning his original scene, he set out at once to capture this feeling, using a nearby grove and swamp as his subject. More often the mood possesses him long before he begins to paint. When it grows strong enough, he starts looking, driving to half-remembered spots, exploring new roads in search of the right setting. One afternoon, on such a quest, he

Sigh of September Wind. 1954. Conté crayon. 10⅞ x 17. Collection of the artist.

thought he had found what he wanted. "I studied the field hard, trying to 'see' it as a subject, but could not. A short walk down to a crossroads, and here I found what I was looking for—a nondescript scene but having the quality of something ancient . . . a dirt crossroads under a still, hot July sun." One of his finest pictures of the last five years, *An April Mood*, was born this way. Early in 1946, he conceived the idea of a bleak landscape expressive of "the anger of God—a Good Friday mood." He found his subject in the country below Boston, where he made his first studies on "a dark lowery day with scudding clouds and only momentary gleams of pale sunshine. Snow squalls at times. . . . A sketch of the sky and old maple trees on edge of a woods." The season passed, so he put the picture aside. Two springs later, he took it out again, studied it and made a number of changes. The following April he worked on it once more, briefly but with great concentration. It was nearly finished, but the last touches were not put on until the spring of 1955, nine years after it had been started. The long process had been necessary to distill the bitter mood he sought. And it is significant of the change that had come over him that this had been achieved not by an arbitrary symbol of God's wrath, however inventive or evocative that might have been, but rather by a powerful metamorphosis of nature, by the gaunt trees, the heavy rocks, the great ragged circle of clouds in the sky, the somber grays tinged with green, all knit together in a brooding design of mighty thrusts and counterthrusts.

Not all Burchfield's recent work has achieved such intensity, nor has it all followed this stylistic direction. He is still drawn at times toward a more fantastic approach and still uses abstract conventionalizations occasionally, like those in *March Wind, Oncoming Spring* and *Hot September Wind*. But these pictures are, themselves, more abstract throughout and therefore more consistent pictorially. In most of his recent fantasies, moreover, he has avoided any obvious symbolism and has been content to deal imaginatively with natural forms, altering their scale and normal relations, somewhat as he had done in 1916 but in the more painterly style of his maturity. Pictures like *Winter Moonlight, Pussy Willows in the Rain* and *Moonflowers at Dusk* evoke their moods by a selective process that magnifies and underlines natural effects, rather than by abstract conventions. The word fantasy scarcely applies to them any more.

There have also been moments in the last few years when Burchfield wondered, "Is realism, after all, better than imaginative invention? What more beautiful than just these delicate trees against the moonlit sky, reproduced just about as they are?" Certain subjects have delighted him so much that he has painted them for themselves rather than as the vehicle of a mood. This was the case with the deserted grange hall in *Old Meeting House and Locust Trees*, which he discovered late one afternoon in 1952. Returning the next day, he painted it rapidly, then worried lest he had been too violent in his treatment of the majestic trees, for this was not intended to be a fantasy. Yet the interesting thing is that the picture does actually approach his more

Spring Rain in the Marsh. 1950/54. India ink, watercolor wash, conté crayon. 11 x 17. Collection of Mr. and Mrs. B. J. Cutler.

fanciful style, as if the latter had become an integral part of his vision and the movements of his hand. The same trend can be seen in a number of other pictures, such as *Still Life in Winter, Hepatica Hollow* and *Windblown Hemlock*, apparently realist in intent but plainly marked with abstract improvisations. So it is apparent that, just as the imaginative paintings have become less fantastic, those done entirely from nature have become more so, and the diverse strands of Burchfield's art have been woven closer.

This more unified style springs basically from Burchfield's surer knowledge of his own powers and his own direction, a knowledge that is reflected in many of the journal entries. He has learned, for instance, to accept certain limitations on his art. Looking at the falls and ravine in Letchworth Park, he concluded that they were "on too overwhelming a scale for intimate interpretation." Other subjects he has come to reject because they are too easy. Sketching near Lime Lake one day, he "spent about a quarter hour planning and mentally painting the little scene to the west. . . . But I had to give it up as not being different enough, it seemed I had done it all before. . . . It probably has too much charm." And he has learned that not all moods are paintable. Once, in an hour of depression, he sought to embody that line of the Psalm, "Out of the depths I cry to thee." His subject was a deep ravine with light filtering down through the trees. "But I think I arrived at another mood, a spiritual quality perhaps but one only of deep mystery. There are moods that cannot be translated into visual art." Such limitations do not in any way constrict his art, for they still leave him an inexhaustible field that he has made his own—the intimate interpretation of all nature. And no other American artist, since the mid-nineteenth century, has approached nature more closely, expressed her moods more imaginatively, or found in her presence a greater spiritual force.

Youth is perennial in Burchfield. One November night in 1952 he stood on a hilltop watching the moon rise, facing a gusty southeast wind that tugged at his clothes. A sense of renewal swept over him, "years seemed to drop away, and I felt the eternal youth of the spirit that never need leave us, in spite of bodily decay, if only we keep our minds and hearts pure and in tune with our Creator. It is not easy to achieve—tonight I felt strong and free, and the whole secret of it seemed to be in the persistent southeast wind." Three days later he was struck by a violent and crippling attack of lumbago, accompanied by intense vertigo and nausea. It was not until the end of February that he could paint in the country again, and he has been hampered ever since by the rigid back-brace that he has to wear. Yet it has never occurred to Burchfield to avoid the now doubled hardships that are the price of reaching those remote spots where nature reveals to him most clearly the wonder and mystery of the universe. A little over a year ago, he carried three loads of painting equipment deep into a ravine and was so exhausted that he had to lie long on the ground before he could start working. Yet, "I had wanted to paint just like this —under the most trying conditions—to prove to myself I could still do it. What will I do when at last I am too old to work under such stress? I think perhaps," he concluded, "I will try it anyhow, and gladly accept the risk of dying in the attempt."

BIBLIOGRAPHY AND INDEX

SELECTED BIBLIOGRAPHY

The place of publication of books is New York unless otherwise noted. The place of publication of periodicals has not been noted, with a few exceptions.

Abbreviations: Ag August, Am American, Ap April, bibl bibliography, bul bulletin, D December, ed edited, F February, il illustration(s), Ja January, Je June, Jl July, mag magazine, Mr March, My May, N November, O October, p page(s), S September, sup supplement.

WRITINGS BY BURCHFIELD

Foreword. *Charles Burchfield,* 1945 [see bibl. below].

Hopper: Career of Silent Poetry. *Art News* 49:14-17,62-4 Mr 1950.

Edward Hopper — Classicist. Museum of Modern Art: *Edward Hopper Retrospective Exhibition,* 1933, p16.

Henry G. Keller. *Am. Mag. of Art* 29:586-93 S 1936.

Norman Kent's Wood Blocks. *Print Connoisseur* 9:313-21 O 1929.

Metropolitan Prospectus: Pro & Con. [Letter to the Editor.] *Art Digest* 26:4 S 15 1952.

On the Middle Border. *Creative Art* 3:xxii-xxxii S 1928. 7 il.

Eugene Speicher. Albright Art Gallery: *Eugene Speicher,* 1950, p9-12. Also in The Century Association, N. Y.: *Eugene Speicher,* 1951-52, [p6-9].

Sun and Rocks. *Albright Art Gallery. Gallery Notes* 18:24-5 Ja 1954. 1 il.

BOOKS

Albright Art Gallery, Buffalo: *Catalogue of Contemporary Paintings and Sculpture,* ed. by Andrew C. Ritchie, 1949, p28-9. 1 il.

Baur, John I. H.: *Revolution and Tradition in Modern American Art,* Cambridge, 1951, p20,28,92-3, 96, 114-6,131. 3 il.

Boswell, Peyton, Jr.: *Modern American Painting,* 1939, p57,79,130. 2 il.

Brown, Milton W.: *American Painting from the Armory Show to the Depression,* Princeton, 1955, p173-81. 6 il.

Charles Burchfield, American Artists Group, 1945. 57 il.

Burroughs, Alan: *Limners and Likenesses,* Cambridge, 1936, p211,213-14,216. 1 il.

Cahill, Holger, and Barr, Alfred H., Jr., ed.: *Art in America in Modern Times,* 1934, p40,95. 1 il.

Cheney, Martha Candler: *Modern Art in America,* 1939, p15,122,125-6. 1 il.

Craven, Thomas: *Famous Artists and Their Models,* 1949, p123-5. 1 il.

—————— *Modern Art,* 1934, p315,328-9. 1 il.

—————— ed.: *A Treasury of Art Masterpieces,* 1939, p574-5. 1 il.

Current Biography, 1942, p114-16. 1 il.

Flexner, James Thomas: *The Pocket History of American Painting,* 1950, p100-01,115. 1 il.

Goodrich, Lloyd: *American Watercolor and Winslow Homer,* Minneapolis, 1945, p79-86. 7 il.

Hall, W. S.: *Eyes on America,* 1939, p25,49,75,80,92. 5 il.

Larkin, Oliver W.: *Art and Life in America,* 1949, p381-2,426-8. 2 il.

Mellquist, Jerome: *The Emergence of an American Art,* 1942, p300-2.

Myers, Bernard S., ed.: *Encyclopedia of Painting,* 1955, p61. 1 il.

Pagano, Grace: *The Encyclopaedia Britannica Collection of Contemporary American Painting,* Chicago, 1946, 2 il.

Robb, David M.: *The Harper History of Painting,* 1951, p927-8. 1 il.

Saint-Gaudens, Homer: *The American Artist and His Times,* 1941, p281-2. 1 il.

Soby, James Thrall: *Contemporary Painters,* 1948, p21-7. 2 il.

Watson, Forbes: *American Painting Today,* 1939, p38-9. 3 il.

Zigrosser, Carl: *The Artist in America,* 1942, p183-4.

EXHIBITION CATALOGUES

Albright Art Gallery, Buffalo: *Charles Burchfield,* introduction by A. C. Ritchie, 1944. 54 il.

Brooklyn Museum: *Revolution and Tradition,* by John I. H. Baur, 1951-52. 1 il.

Carnegie Institute: *Survey of American Painting,* 1940. 1 il.

—————— *Water Colors and Oils by Charles Burchfield,* 1938. 3 il.

Cleveland Museum of Art: *The Drawings of Charles E. Burchfield,* 1953. 21 il.

Galerie de la Chambre Syndicale des Beaux-Arts, Paris: *Exhibition of American Art,* [1924]. 1 il.

Institute of Contempoary Art, Boston: *Milestones of American Painting in Our Century,* by Frederick S. Wight, 1949, p68-9. 1 il.

Kevorkian Galleries, N.Y.: *Drawings in Watercolor by Charles Burchfield,* 1920. 11 il.

Metropolitan Museum of Art: *The Edward Root Collection,* 1953.

Musée National d'Art Moderne, Paris: 50 *Ans d'Art aux Etats-Unis. Collections du Museum of Modern Art de New York,* 1955, p21,39. 1 il.

Museum of Fine Arts, Boston: *Ten American Watercolor Painters,* 1939, p7.

Museum of Modern Art, N.Y.: *Charles Burchfield. Early Watercolors,* 1930. 10 il.

———*Paintings by Nineteen Living Americans,* 1929-30, p12-13,15. 2 il.

——— *Romantic Painting in America,* by James Thrall Soby and Dorothy C. Miller, 1943, p42,131. 3 il.

Newark Museum: *American Paintings and Sculpture from the Museum's Collections,* introduction by Holger Cahill, 1944-45, p48,95,173. 1 il.

PERIODICALS

Abbott, Jere: Burchfield and Sheeler for the U.S. Collection at Smith College. *Art News* 39:6,12,17 D 14 1940. 1 il.

——— Moving Day. *Smith College Museum Bul.* 22:7-9 Je 1941. 1 il.

Activity: Birge and Burchfield. *Mag. of Art* 31:44 Ja 1938. 2 il.

Art: *Bulletin Index,* Pittsburgh, 112:17 Mr 24 1938. 1 il.

Art. *Time* 24:25 D 24, 1934. 2 il.

——— 47:61 Ja 21, 1946. 3 il.

——— 60:89 N 24 1952. 1 il.

——— 60:76-7 D 8 1952. 1 il.

Artist. *Buffalo Business* 16:14-15 Jl 1942. 3 il.

Barker, Virgil: Notes on the Exhibitions. *Arts* 5:218-19 Ap 1924. 2 il.

Benson, E. M.: The American Scene. *Am. Mag. of Art* 27:61,64-5 F 1934. 2 il.

Bird, Paul: The Fortnight in New York. *Art Digest* 11:18 D 1 1936. 1 il.

Boswell, Peyton: American Art as it is Today. *Studio* 113:28 Ja 1937. 1 il.

Bredemeier, Carl: Charles Burchfield "The Honest." *Buffalo Arts Journal* 8:15-16 Summer 1926. 3 il.

Breuning, Margaret: Current Exhibitions. *Parnassus* 8:31 D 1936.

Brown, Milton W.: The Early Realism of Hopper and Burchfield. *College Art Journal* 7:3-11 Autumn 1947. 2 il.

Buffalo Reviews Art of Burchfield. *Art Digest* 18:6 Ap 15 1944. 2 il.

Charles Burchfield. *Art News* 30:10 O 31 1931.

Burchfield Exhibition Rated a "Knockout." *Art Digest* 16:7 N 1 1941. 1 il.

Burchfield Explains. *Art Digest* 19:56 Ap 1 1945.

A Burchfield for Syracuse. *Art Digest* 11:16 My 1 1937.

Charles E. Burchfield—Painter. *Index of Twentieth Century Artists* 2no3:37-40 sup i-ii D 1934.

Burchfield, Painter of Weather, Exhibits Latest Watercolors. *Art Digest* 13:7 Ja 1 1939. 1 il.

A Burchfield Water Color. *Albright Art Gallery. Gallery Notes.* 11:11-12, 16 Jl 1946. 1 il.

Burchfield's America. *Life* 1:24-9 D 28 1936. 11 il.

Burchfield's Buffalo. *Art News* 43:12-13 My 1 1944. 8 il.

Burchfield, Louise H.: Retrospective Exhibition of Paintings by Charles Burchfield. *Cleveland Museum of Art Bul.* 32:8-9 Ja 1945.

——— A Water Color by Charles Burchfield. *Cleveland Museum of Art Bul.* 25:66,71 Ap 1938. 1 il.

By Henry McBride. *Art News* 49:47 My 1950.

——— 51:47 D 1952.

Cahill, Holger: In Our Time. *Mag. of Art* 39:316 N 1946. 1 il.

Campbell, Lawrence: Charles Burchfield [In "Reviews and Previews."] *Art News* 53:50 D 1954.

Carnegie Institute Picks Jurors for "American Directions" Show. *Art Digest* 15:12 Jl 1 1941. 1 il.

Citations. *Hamilton [College] Alumni Review* 13:181-2 Jl 1948. 1 il.

Coates, Robert M.: The Art Galleries. *New Yorker* 23:97 O 18 1947.

Craven, Thomas: American Painting. *Studio* 127:173,176 Je 1944. 1 il.

——— Our Art Becomes American. *Harper's Mag.* 171:433 S 1935.

Current Exhibitions of Interest. *Parnassus* 2:3, 6-7 Ap 1930. 1 il.

D. D.: Burchfield: Pougialis. *Art News* 34:6 O 26 1935. 1 il.

M.D.: Charles Burchfield. [In "New Exhibitions of the Week."] *Art News* 37:13 Ja 7 1939.

——— Burchfield's Landscapes. [In "New Exhibitions of the Week."] *Art News* 35:18 N 21 1936.

Davis, Clyde Brion: Buffalo. *Holiday* 18:98 Ag 1955. 1 il.

Devree, Howard: Around New York. [In "Exhibition Reviews."] *Mag. of Art* 32:100-01 F 1939.

———Burchfield, Bacon, McFee. [In "Seeing the Shows."] *Mag. of Art* 30:51 Ja 1937.

S.F.: Charles Burchfield. *Arts Digest* 29:23 N 15 1954. 1 il.

Field Notes. *Am. Mag. of Art* 27:492,498 S 1934. 1 il.

Fitzsimmons, James: Nature Interpreted. *Art Digest* 27:16 N 15 1952. 1 il.

[Five illustrations.] *Dial* 68:478 Ap 1920.

Friends of Art Buy a Burchfield. *Art Digest* 16:7 D 15 1941. 1 il.

Furst, Herbert: Burchfield. *Apollo* 40:124-5 N 1944.

Genauer, Emily: Cover Painting, *What's New,* Chicago, 184:13 Fall 1954. 1 il.

Gibbs, Jo: Burchfield Reverts Back to Early Fantasy. *Art Digest* 20:9 Ja 1 1946. 2 il.

Gift to Carnegie. *Art Digest* 19:7 Ja 1 1945. 1 il.

"Glory to God" by Burchfield. *Lutheran Witness* 72:2 N 24 1953. 1 il.

Goodrich, Lloyd: New York Exhibitions. *Arts* 9:226-7 Ap 1926. 1 il.

Hale, Robert Beverly: The Growth of a Collection. *Metropolitan Museum of Art Bul.* 11:154,160 F 1953. 1 il.

Hopper, Edward: Charles Burchfield. *Arts* 14:5-12 Jl 1928. 6 il.

Edward Hopper Objects. *Art of Today* 6:11 F 1935.

Jewell, Edward Alden: American Painting. *Creative Art* 9:365-6 N 1931. 1 il.

F.L.K.: Burchfield, Painter of Familiar Scenes. *Survey Graphic* 14:159-61 N 1928. 6 il.

Krasne, Belle: A Charles Burchfield Profile. *Art Digest* 27:9,21-2 D 15 1952. 2 il.

Kretzmann, Adalbert R.: Charles Ephraim Burchfield. *Cresset,* Minneapolis, 8:33-40 Mr 1945. 7 il.

J.L.: Romantic Early Papers by Burchfield. *Art News* 38:10 D 9 1939.

Letters and Art. *Literary Digest* 120:18 O 19 1935. 1 il.

Lyle, Henry H. M.: Charles Burchfield, American. *Charaka Club Proceedings,* N. Y., 8:135-9 1935. 4 il.

McBride, Henry: Burchfield. *Creative Art* 3:xxxii S 1928.
_____ Modern Art. *Dial* 72:437-8 Ap 1922.
_____ 76:478 My 1924. 1 il.

McCausland, Elizabeth: Exhibitions in New York. *Parnassus* 11:22 D 1939.

McCormick, William B.: A Small Town in Paint. *International Studio* 80:466-70 Mr 1925. 6 il.

Mann, Marty: Exhibitions. *International Studio* 96:94 My 1930. 1 il.
_____ Through the Galleries. *Town and Country* 85:115-16 My 1 1930. 1 il.

Mannes, Marya: News of the Month. *Creative Art* 2:XLVII My 1928. 1 il.

Morsell, Mary: Modern Museum Exhibits the Art of Sixteen Cities. *Art News* 32:13 D 23 1933. 1 il.

Mumford, Lewis: The Art Galleries. *New Yorker* 10:49-50 F 24 1934.
_____ 11:40 N 2 1935.
_____ 12:91 N 28 1936.

Muskegon Buys Burchfield and Curry Works. *Art Digest* 10:16 O 1 1935. 1 il.

New York Criticism. *Art Digest* 8:14 Mr 1 1934.
_____ 10:18 N 1 1935.

New York Season. *Art Digest* 4:16 Ap 1 1930.
_____ 6:23 N 15 1931.

O'Connor, John, Jr.: Charles Burchfield. *Carnegie Mag.* 11:309-12 Mr 1938. 3 il.

_____ Directions in American Painting. *Carnegie Mag.* 15:89-90 Je 1941. 1 il.
_____ Jury of Award. *Carnegie Mag.* 24:418-19 S 1950. 1 il.
_____ Painting Presented to the Carnegie Institute. *Carnegie Mag.* 18:201-4 D 1944. 1 il.
_____ Two Burchfields Are Given. *Carnegie Mag.* 20:104-6 O 1946. 2 il.

On View in the New York Galleries. *Parnassus* 2:6 D 1930.

Parks, Robert O.: Road in Early Spring. *Art Association of Indianapolis Bul.* 30:16-17 Je 1943. 1 il.

The Passing Shows. *Art News* 42:21 N 1 1943.
_____ 44:26 Ja 1 1946. 1 il.

Pemberton, Murdock: The Art Galleries. *New Yorker* 3:45 F 4 1928.

The Pennsylvania Academy's One Hundred and Twenty-fourth Annual Exhibition. *Am. Mag. of Art* 20:138,141 Mr 1929. 1 il.

Philadelphia: Mexican Lithography & Burchfield Watercolors. *Art News* 36:17-18 N 6 1937.

Phillips, Duncan: Original American Painting of Today. *Formes* 21:200 Ja 1932. 1 il.

Pittsburgh: A Comprehensive Showing of the Work of Burchfield. *Art News* 36:18 Ap 2 1938. 1 il.

Pousette-Dart, Nathaniel: Charles Burchfield. *Studio News* 5:6-7 Ap 1934. 2 il.

Prasse, Leona E.: An Exhibition of the Drawings of Charles E. Burchfield. *Cleveland Museum of Art Bul.* 40:203-4 N 1953. 1 il.

Read, Helen Appleton: Charles Burchfield. *Studio* 116:208-11 O 1938. 5 il.

Reed, Judith Kaye: Burchfield Finds Beauty in His Mother Lode. *Art Digest* 22:21 O 15 1947. 1 il.

Reviews & Previews. *Art News* 46:42-3 N 1947.

Richardson, E. P.: Charles Burchfield. *Mag. of Art* 37:208-12 O 1944. 5 il.
_____ Painting in America: The Historian's Problem. *Art Quarterly* 14:336 Winter 1951. 1 il.
_____ Watercolor: The American Medium? *Art News* 44:22,29,30 Ap 15 1945. 1 il.

Riley, Maude: Burchfield Exhibits Latest Watercolors. *Art Digest* 18:11 N 1 1943. 1 il.

Rogers, Meyric R.: Three Contemporary American Paintings. *City Art Museum of St. Louis Bul.* 21:71 O 1936.

Rothenstein, John: Painting in America. *Horizon,* London, 3:415 Je 1941. 1 il.

Rowland, Benjamin, Jr.: Burchfield's Seasons. *Fogg Museum of Art Bul.* 10:155-61 N 1946. 3 il.

J. S.: Charles Burchfield. *Art News* 32:13 F 10 1934.

A Sad Note Creeps Into Burchfield's Art. *Art Digest* 8:16 F 15 1934. 1 il.

Sharp, Marynell: New Burchfields. *Art Digest* 24:10 Ap 15 1950. 1 il.

Sweeney, James Johnson: L'art contemporain aux Etats-Unis. *Cahiers d'Art* no1-2: 52,64 1938. 1 il.

Vanishing Backyards. *Fortune* 1:77,80-1 My 1930. 3 il.

Watson, Ernest W.: Charles Burchfield. *Am. Artist* 6:4-11 My 1942. 18 il.

Watson, Forbes: In the Galleries. *Arts* 16:578,584 Ap 1930. 1 il.

Watson, Jane: News and Comment: Hopper on Burchfield. *Mag. of Art* 34:344,381 Ag 1941. 1 il.

When Burchfield Was a Young Romantic. *Art Digest* 14:6 D 1 1939. 1 il.

Whiting, F. A., Jr.: A Note on Burchfield. *Mag. of Art* 30:352 Je 1937. 1 il.

INDEX

PLATES

1. Rogues' Gallery

1916. Watercolor. 13½ x 19⅝. Museum of Modern Art, gift of Mrs. John D. Rockefeller, Jr.

A rogues' gallery of sunflowers in the brilliant, dry sunshine of August.

2. Church Bells Ringing, Rainy Winter Night

1917. Watercolor. 30 x 19. Cleveland Museum of Art, anonymous gift in memory of Henry G. Keller.

It was an attempt to express a childhood emotion—a rainy winter night—the churchbell is ringing and it terrifies me (the child)—the bell ringing motive reaches out and saturates the rainy sky—the roofs of the houses dripping with rain are influenced; the child attempts to be comforted by the thoughts of candle lights and Christmas trees, but the fear of the black, rainy night is overpowering.

3. Ghost Plants

1916. 20 x 14. Collection of Mr. and Mrs. Kenneth M. Parker.

4. Setting Sun through the Catalpas

1916. 20¼ x 14¼. Cleveland Museum of Art, Hinman B. Hurlbut Collection.

5. Poplars in June

1917. 18 x 22. Collection of the artist.

6. The Window by the Alley

1917. 18 x 24¾. Collection of Mr. and Mrs. Andrew C. Ritchie.

7. The Mysterious Bird

1917. Watercolor. 20¾ x 17⅝. Wilmington Society of the Fine Arts.

A bird kept going back and forth overhead making a strange whistling sound. I never could catch a look at him—he remained merely a sound.

8. Dandelion Seed Balls and Trees

1917. 22¼ x 18¼. Metropolitan Museum of Art.

9. Garden of Memories

1917. Watercolor and crayon. 25¾ x 22½. Museum of Modern Art, gift of Mrs. John D. Rockefeller, Jr.

Crabbed old age sits in front of her black doorway, without hope for the future, brooding. Spiders lurk
in dark corners; the dying plants reflect her mood. The romantic autumn moon rises just the same.

10. Portrait Study in a Doorway

1917. Gouache. 24 x 30. Phillips Collection, Washington, D. C.

Not an attempt to produce a "bona fide" portrait, but merely a study of a mood in which the figure is simply one of many objects.

12. The Song of the Katydids

1917. Watercolor. 17¾ x 21¾. Collection of Mr. and Mrs. Lawrence A. Fleischman.

A stagnant August morning during the drought season; as the pitiless sun mounts into the midmorning sky the insect chorus commences, the katydids and locusts predominating; their monotonous, mechanical, brassy rhythms soon pervade the whole air, combining with heat waves of the sun, and saturating trees and houses and sky.

11. Insects at Twilight

1917. 14 x 19¾.
Museum of Modern Art, gift of
Mrs. John D.
Rockefeller, Jr.

12

13. The Night Wind

1918. Watercolor.
21¼ x 21¾. Collection of
A. Conger Goodyear.

To the child sitting cozily in his
home, the roar of the wind
outside fills his mind full of visions
of strange phantoms and monsters
flying over the land.

14

15

14. Black Houses

1918. Watercolor. 16 x 24⅝. Collection of Mr. and Mrs. Theodor Braasch.

Crude frame houses rearing themselves up against the cold afterglow in the western sky, like gaunt black spectres which seem to be resisting the light with all the bulky power they can muster. They are symbols of the hardness of life, and are also beautiful in their primitive, almost elemental conception of the idea of "homes."

15. White Violets and Coal Mine

1918. Watercolor. 23¼ x 21¼. Cleveland Museum of Art, Hinman B. Hurlbut Collection.

The debris at the mine openings seemed to be especially suitable for white violets, delicate fragile flowers, whose charm was enhanced by the proximity of the yawning black cave, around which they grew. They seemed like impish fairy spirits playing hide-and-seek among the rocks.

16. Cricket Chorus in the Arbor

1917. Watercolor. 22 x 18. Collection of John W. Straus.

With the afterglow reflected in the southeast sky, the cricket chorus commences in the black depths of the forest.

17. Haunted Evening

1919. Watercolor. 16 x 25. Collection of Mr. and Mrs. Henry E. Richter.

A reminiscence of South Carolina where I spent six months in the Army. . . .
A man coming home to his little cabin, carrying his sack of provender, fearful
of the eerie, haunted, skull-like woods that stands behind his home, against a
lurid sunset sky.

18. Wires Down

1920. Watercolor. 19 x 31⅛. Carnegie Institute, gift of Mrs. James H.
Beal, Jr.

It is exhilarating to go out on such a morning and feel the cold damp air, and
observe the strange white light that glows at the horizon against which the
wet houses are dark geometric-shaped blots.

19. The Thunderclap

1920. Gouache. 26 x 40. Collection of the artist.

My aim was to create, if possible, the feeling that this perhaps could have been the very first thunderclap that rolled across the world after the Creation. . . . An elemental world fashioned from the very reverberations from the booming thunder, a world bronzed by the heat and drought of August.

20. Noonday Heat

1921. Varnished watercolor. 22 x 32. Collection of Mrs. George Bellows.

21. House of Mystery

1924. Varnished watercolor and tempera. 29½ x 24½. Art Institute of Chicago.

What I . . . tried to express was a feeling of deep mystery, that it was a house where anything might have happened, or be happening.

22. March Wind

1926. Watercolor. 26½ x 39¾. Cleveland Museum of Art, J. H. Wade Collection.

The March wind comes up out of the vast southwest . . . over bare brown and gray fields and hillocks . . . over housetops and clusters of farm buildings. The March wind is master over them all—it sweeps along blending all these dissimilar things into one grand harmonious whole.

23. Sulphurous Evening

1922/29. Watercolor. 24 x 30. City Art Museum of St. Louis.

One of those evenings in late August when, following a stormy rainy day, the sun . . . manages to break through at last and fills the whole upper air with an ominous yellow light. Something tremendous, or even disastrous seems about to happen.

24. Rainy Night

1930. Watercolor. 32 x 44. Fine Arts Gallery of San Diego.

A rainy night in a city when the clouds are hanging low. . . . It is only then that the lights . . . are reflected in the sky in such beautiful variations. Wet asphalt reflecting the sky and lights seems to create another infinity below, so that the buildings are poised between two intangible areas, adding mystery to the whole scene.

25. Evening

1932. Watercolor. 31½ x 43½. Newark Museum.

It is not only "Evening" of the day, but also of the year, when Nature is "spent," all her work for the year finished, and the earth is slowly mouldering into decay. ... It is [also] "Evening" in the lives of the three people sitting under the trees. They live alone, all they have left in life are memories. They sit brooding.

26. Winter Bouquet

1933. Watercolor. 36 x 27. Museum of Fine Arts, Boston.

Sometimes it seems to me that certain weeds are more alive when dried than when they were full of sap and growing in the fields. In this painting I have tried to capture the beauty of autumn, bring it into my studio and imprison it, as it were, in a bouquet.

27. March Sunlight

1925/33. Watercolor. 23¼ x 32. Fogg Art Museum, Harvard University.

The effect sought here is of the late afternoon sunlight in early Spring, when young trees seem to bristle with up-shooting growth.... To me the little islands in the center were like a dream world, or fairyland come to life.

28. November Evening

1931-34. Oil. 32⅛ x 52. Metropolitan Museum of Art.

I have attempted to express the coming of winter over the Middle West as it must have felt to the pioneers—great black clouds sweep out of the west at twilight as if to overwhelm not only the pitiful human attempt at a town, but also the earth itself.

30. Black Iron

1935. Watercolor. 29 x 41. Collection of Mr. and Mrs. Lawrence A. Fleischman.

I had observed and admired the two bridges for many years—a wonderful structure of blackness even on the sunniest day, but on a gray day the epitome of sinister darkness. . . . Even the stream below, polluted as it was with various chemicals and oily substances, seemed to be made of liquid black iron.

29. The Parade

1932-34. Watercolor. 26 x 37. Collection of Mr. and Mrs. Lawrence A. Fleischman.

Looking through a viaduct at a communist parade. While the parade establishes the mood, it is readily seen that the big kick to me . . . was trying to express the *hollowness* of the cavities under the viaduct.

31. Six O'Clock

1936. Watercolor. 24 x 30. Syracuse Museum of Fine Arts.

The supper hour in the kitchen of one of a row of identical factory workers' houses. . . . A cozy heart-warming scene which contrasts with the scene outside, where the pale yellow afterglow lights up the faces of the houses and the snowdrifts.

30

31

32. **Old House by Creek**

1932-1938. Oil. 34½ x 57. Whitney Museum of American Art.

One of the things that attracted me to this subject is the manner in which terribly hideous objects are, by being reflected in the oily olive-green water, transformed into shapes of mystery and beauty.

33. End of the Day

1938. Watercolor. 28 x 48. Pennsylvania Academy of the Fine Arts.

At the end of a day of hard labor, the workmen plod wearily uphill in the eerie twilight of winter, and it seems to the superficial eye that they have little to come home to in those stark unpainted houses. But like the houses, they persist and will not give in, and so they attain a rugged dignity that compels our admiration.

34. Edge of Town

1921/41. Watercolor. 27 x 40. Nelson-Atkins Gallery of Art, Kansas City, Mo., gift of the Friends of Art.

An evening in midwinter, at the time when the afterglow of the day and man-made lights strive for the mastery.... In earlier times, small towns seemed sometimes to end abruptly on the very edge of desolation.

35. The Coming of Spring

1917/43. Watercolor. 34 x 48. Metropolitan Museum of Art.

The attempt here was to express ... the contrast of winter and spring by showing two kinds of hollows or ravines.... One was to be dead and lifeless, with ice remnants, and no sign of growth, black and void; the other to be alive with growing things and leading out to a blinding white sky, which was to typify the sun.

36. The Cicada

1944. Watercolor. 30 x 25. Collection of Edward W. Root.

For me, insects have just as much personality as other wild creatures.... The cicada, the soul of midsummer, embodying in its song all the heat and rhythm of a sultry day, when the sun pours down out of a pale hot lavender sky on a parched and drought-ridden earth.

37. The Sphinx and the Milky Way

1946. Watercolor. 52⅝ x 44¾. Munson-Williams-Proctor Institute, Utica.

A summer night–a garden of flowers flanked by a grape arbor. A pale ghostly white nicotiana flower, with a sphinx or hawk moth poised before it with rapidly beating wings, sipping its honey. . . . The air is heavy with flower scents, and filled with the songs of insects.

38. The Three Trees

1932/46. Watercolor. 36 x 60. Salem Public Library, Salem, Ohio.

I have never seen a more noble group of trees, and to me they epitomize all that Salem meant to me as a boy and young man. . . . As an underlying motif, in addition to expressing the mood of childhood when a summer noon seems endless, I have tried to express the idea of the presence of God, the beneficent "God-in-nature" that Beethoven spoke of often.

39. Moonflowers at Dusk

1952. Watercolor. 40 x 33. Collection of Mr. and Mrs. William J. Poplack.

A backyard garden in late summer at twilight.... In the background broods
the northern sky, overcast with a thunderstorm. One of the thunderheads rising
like a pillar against the black sky, is lit up by pale moonlight, complementing
the deep mystery that lurks in the depths of trees and bushes.

40. Hush before the Storm

1947. Watercolor. 40 x 30. Roland P. Murdock Collection, Wichita Art Museum.

Deep mystery lurks in the black interior of the trees, and the feeling of foreboding is emphasized by the startled white daisies in the foreground.

41. Lavender and Old Lace

1939/47. Watercolor. 36¾ x 52½. New Britain Art Museum.

An elegy. The original study for this painting was made on the spot.... Later it was enlarged considerably ... but somehow it seemed to lack either mood or mystery.... [Then] I allowed my imagination to take over.... I changed the time from that of a gray daylight to late twilight. But most important, the huge elm that dominates the background and provides the mood was also added at this time.

42. July Clouds

1948. 26 x 35. Collection of Mr. and Mrs. Walter E. Ferris.

41

42

43. Hot September Wind

1953. Watercolor. 40 x 30. Collection of Mr. and Mrs. Lawrence A. Fleischman.

A hot southwest wind pouring out of the heat-hazed sky, dragging with it streamers of yellow sunlight, sweeps over the woods into the meadow.

44. Clatter of Crows in Spring Woods

1949. Watercolor. 40 x 30. Wolf Collection.

Walking along through a woods in early spring hoping to find the first wildflower; all is quiet, except for the low murmur of a tumbling rill. . . . Suddenly without warning a terrific clatter shatters the silence — a flock of crows has seen the intruder. As they angrily fly away, a cacophonous medley of sound fills the whole woods. One of the most thrilling events in nature.

45. Summer Afternoon

1917/48. Watercolor. 48 x 42. Collection of the artist.

The stream is the Little Beaver Creek. . . . Here as a boy I used to go swimming.
I have tried to express . . . the ineffable peace of a quiet summer day in those far-off
times. All things seem to look at and yearn toward the sun.

46. Sun and Rocks

1918/50. Watercolor. 40 x 56. Room of Contemporary Art Collection, Albright Art Gallery, Buffalo.

An attempt to depict a scene in primeval times, in early spring, when conflicting forces of nature hold sway and seem to fill the earth with violence and chaos. . . . Shining from the deep blue cavernous sky, the spring sun—our great daytime star—floods the scene with brilliant light that will heal the wounds of the earth and bring forth new life.

47. Winter Moonlight

1951. Watercolor. 40 x 33. Roland P. Murdock Collection, Wichita Art Museum.

A calm winter's night in a snowbound woods. The moon, encircled by the large glowing ring that portends change in the weather, lights up the clean white snow.... To the left of the moon are the Pleiades, faintly visible.

49. March Wind

1951; incorrectly dated 1952. Watercolor. 30 x 40. Frank K. M. Rehn Galleries.

Painted in a late winter blizzard.... All the mental work had been completed beforehand, but I think working under such conditions helped me to reduce the "idea of wind" to its simplest, most economical terms.

48. Song of the Marsh

1951. Watercolor. 25 x 36. Collection of Joseph H. Hirshhorn.

From the tangled depths of last year's reeds and cattails . . . ascends the shrill piping song of spring peepers, mingled with the liquid notes of a red-winged blackbird.

49

50. Old Meetinghouse and Locust Trees

1952. Watercolor. 30 x 40. Frank K. M. Rehn Galleries.

A hot afternoon in mid-August. . . . From the trees is heard the persistent rasping rhythms of the songs of cicadas.

51. Song of the Telegraph

1917/52. Watercolor. 34 x 53. Frank K. M. Rehn Galleries.

There are few sounds that are as wild and elemental as this music of the telegraph wires, that stir the blood as much, and fill the listener, boy or man, with such vague but intense yearning for he knows not what.

52. Night of the Equinox

1917/55. Watercolor. 40 x 52. Frank K. M. Rehn Galleries.

One of the most exciting weather events of the whole year was what we called the spring equinoctial storm. . . . It seemed as if terrific forces were abroad in the land. It was delightful, lying there in bed with a sense of cozy security, to imagine that outside fearful monsters were at war with each other.

51

52

53. An April Mood

1946/55. Watercolor. 40 x 54. Whitney Museum of American Art, gift of Mr. and Mrs. Lawrence A. Fleischman and purchase.

A mood embodying the anger of God, frowning on a delinquent mankind . . . [but] the idea changed, or rather expanded to express a general mood of nature. . . . It represents the ever recurrent struggle for supremacy between winter and spring. . . . To the experienced weather eye, there is snow in the threatening overhanging clouds, and spring will retreat again for a time.

54. The Glory of Spring

1934/55. Watercolor. 43 x 54. Frank K. M. Rehn Galleries.

These are the things I love about early spring, and this is the kind of place I love. It is not a particular spot, but the synthesis of all such neglected places.